You Can't Run Away From You

A Young Man's Journey to Himself

Anthony Brinkley

DARNELL PUBLISHING ♦ TAMPA, FL

Published by Darnell Publishing
11705 Boyette Road, Suite 442
Riverview, FL 33569
Amazon.com or
wwwchiefanthonybrinkley.com

Copyright © 2003 by Anthony Brinkley

All rights reserved, including the right of reproduction in whole or in part in any from, except by newspaper or magazine reviewers who wish to quote brief passages in connection with a review. No other part of this publication may be reproduced, stored in a retrieval system, or transmitted in any form or by any means, electronic, mechanical, photocopying, recording, or otherwise without the prior written or expressed permission of Darnell Publishing or Anthony Brinkley, or its assigned agents, or representatives.

Cover Design by Essex James of EJ Graphics
Editing, layout and design by Angela Judge of NdueCzon Publishing Group

Library of Congress Catalog Number available from publisher upon request.

ISBN 978-0-9755616-3-8

Printed in the United States of America
A Darnell Publishing Book
First Edition: November 2020

DEDICATION

I dedicate this work to my mother, Maliscy Brinkley, who is the inspiration for my life and the only example to look towards for womanhood. I would also like to acknowledge Luther, Bowser, aka Chick. Although Chick passed away well before his time, he was like a father to me. My cousin Mark Simms was my protector, mentor, and role model. Mark will always hold a place in my heart and soul. My brother John Brinkley was not the brother I wanted, he was the brother I needed, he helped me transition from a boy to a man, and I am better because of his consistent influence. My father, also known as Mickey, who you will read about in these pages had a profound impact on my life. Although we had a complicated relationship, time has revealed the significance of his impact on me and my orientation to myself and the world. To Matthew and Eva James, they became my spiritual parents and continue to demonstrate unconditional love to me.

My faith as a Christian has sustained me through many dark times, and forged the elements that kept me when I literally wanted to give up on myself. I am living proof that all things are possible if we just trust God. My friend and mentor Isaac Henderson who helped restore my faith in Jesus hovers over my life like an angel and I thank him for his loyalty and support. My inspiration for writing came from a dear friend, Diane Jackson, who pushed me to get started on this journey. I truly understand that I am here because many people took to the time to love, understand, and speak into my life. For all of you who did this I simply say thank you.

PROLUGUE

As I begin to work on this book, our world is in a state of flux. There are wars, as well as rumors of wars. There is the Coronavirus that has become a global pandemic. If we believed everything going on the news, we'd simply bury your heads in the sand and give up. Our world as we know it has become challenged and now people are looking for clarity and comfort. That's why this book will be one that I believe is timely, you see the substance of my platform for resilience and crisis management were forged through devastating circumstances.

Yet, these circumstances or the ones that you may be experiencing can help be the training platform that launches you from a victim mentality to a victor mentality. As I believe these global issues will soon subside, the situations in your life will subside as well if you choose to embrace your challenges and let them develop you and not define you.

Even as I type these pages many in our country are in a sequestered state. Our social interactions have been significantly limited and now each of us will need to examine our true foundation to determine if we are standing on solid ground or on sand. Trust me, this too shall pass and your story is in the midst of being developed.

FOREWORD

Some have said that life is a series of moments strung together. No matter how good or bad the moment is there will be another moment right around the corner, which represents a chance for change. One key to living life versus surviving is to be able to understand the difference between vision and sight. This understanding can be a liberating truth leading the visionary to greater plateaus and living life to the greatest extent. A person who functions by sight gathers their information and direction from external sources. Doing this can lead to misplaced or diminished hopes. More importantly, fashioning one's hopes only on the external gives away too much of what we through the leading of God can contribute to ourselves, as well as others.

I heard of a certain turtle that forages around for food, and if this turtle wanders into a tree, it will die of starvation. All this turtle has to do is lift its head up and go around the tree to continue its quest. So many of us are like that turtle; walking blindly into whatever situation that comes up. If we just simply adjust the way we look at things, and are willing to try a different route, the result can only improve. The Bible puts it best when it says, "Where there is no vision the people perish." My community represents a place where many promising people never realized their true place in the world because of lack of vision and believing the only way to get ahead was by holding someone else back.

One's hopes are not and should not be based on things seen, but should be based on things known in one's heart and spirit. Doing this will help free people from being drowned by the world and its material trappings. How can you explain a person who came from poverty and despair to ascend to a place where no one saw them going? This person did not let the things seen limit their heart or spirit, the drive that motivates this person is not sight but is truly vision.

Vision unlike sight comes from within and is tucked safely in a place that cannot be damaged or influenced by what one sees; thereby; keeping one on the road even when what lies before one's view is bad or appears invincible. No matter the obstacle, vision continues to reach and strive when sight says stop. Vision says yes when the world says no. Vision reminds sight that what a person sees in the physical is just an obstacle to overcome. Overcoming the physical limitations is necessary if one is ever to reach the vision in their heart that their eyes cannot see.

The Bible talks about how the 'just shall walk by faith and not by sight;' this is clearly a reference to having a vision. Vision helps people succeed in spite of circumstances. One has to visualize a place that no one can see in the natural and be prepared to walk towards this destiny. Vision is one of the greatest resources anyone has available. If used, it propels one to overcome no matter what occurs around him or her.

As a man, I had to learn how to break away from traditional views of manhood and what people consider as signs of strength in a man. I now recognize that my strength comes from being secure with me no matter what others think. My strength comes from acknowledging my vision and not from what I see. I was never sure of my feelings or my ability to communicate them until I became secure in this knowledge. The following documents my travels to myself. I challenge you to do what many dare not to, look at who you are with a critical eye. Once you have done that, ask yourself the following questions: Do I follow sight or vision? Am I willing to take the road less traveled that will lead to my destiny?

I invite you to journey with me on the expedition to discover me, to discover my vision, to discover my strength as I live out my destiny.

♦ ♦ ♦ ♦ ♦ ♦

WHEN I WAS A CHILD,
I SPAKE AS A CHILD,
UNDERSTOOD AS A CHILD, …

PHASE I

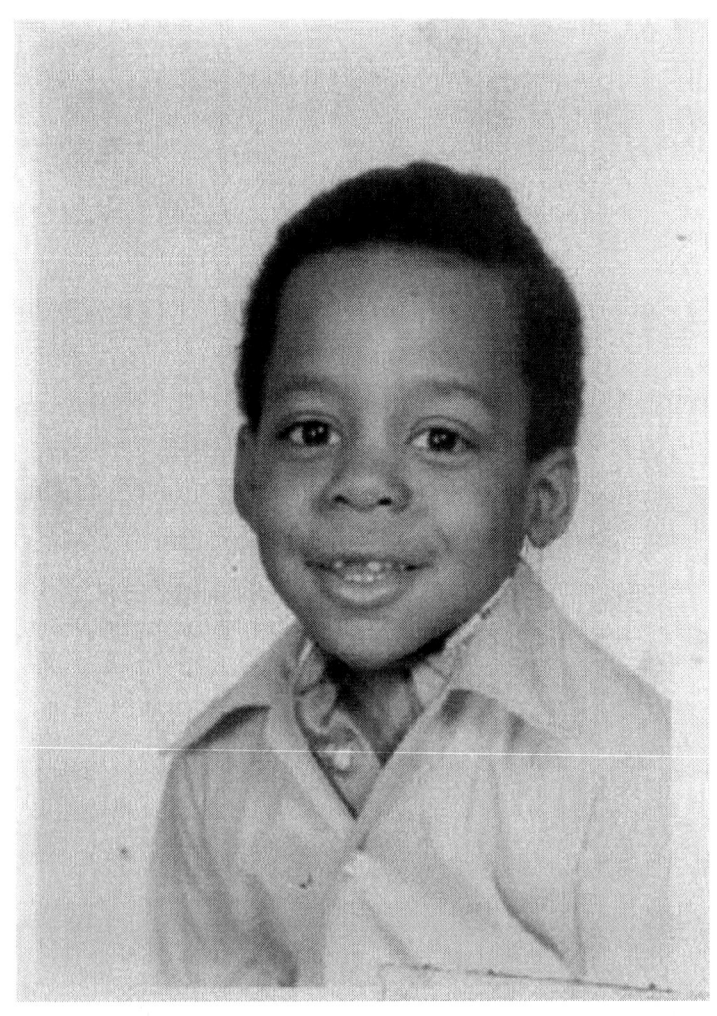

Young Anthony

CHAPTER ONE
ADAPTING TO CHANGE

My first memories in life are mostly of dreams of being in different places and experiencing new things. Even to this day, I dream about new places and experiences. I begin this writing in Korea, a place I never thought that I'd return, because I faced many of my most challenging times here. Although I couldn't tell it at the time, I've learned many lessons from these challenges, so, I don't want to use this time to just tell you a good story. Even though I am still young, I'm sure that woven in all of the adventures I've experienced are some lessons hidden in plain view.

My life began simply enough in Weldon, North Carolina, a town so small that everyone knew one another and seemed like all of us had some sort of family connection. Before I could take it all in, my family moved to Stamford, Connecticut. Stamford, now famous for its "suburban living," was the place I called home for my first 18 years.

Although my early school day experiences were so long ago, I do remember the feeling I had about kindergarten. Going to school was something new and exciting and kindergarten is where it all started. There I got the chance to be with other children. I felt like I was a part of a larger family, felt like I had more brothers than just Joey. Even felt like I had some sisters, too.

Back in the late 60's in Stamford, there was great emphasis placed on making sure each student was prepared in all ways for school. I can remember each of us got a lot of individualized attention. The teachers always made sure we had eaten well during our lunch periods, and those working in the office were busy making sure everything from attendance to current medical records were closely monitored.

Getting shots was the thing I dreaded most back then. But I had little choice because it was either the needle or Mom's belt. What's a kid to do? The needle won out every time. It seemed like the nurse was always coming around to test us for different things, so it became something that all the children learned to tolerate. Notice I didn't say 'got used to,' because we never got used to all the pinching, jabbing, sticking, and stinging. Overall, the adjustment to the school environment was okay. I think all of the playtime had a lot to do with it and I even began to make some friends. One day during that time stands out to me particularly. That day will always be etched in my mind.

As usual, I got up, washed off and rushed to eat my cereal, then hurried to get ready to leave for school. I was around five years old by now and this had become my daily routine. But, on this day, instead of going to school, I remember my mother saying that my brother and I were going for a ride. Now what kid wouldn't be excited about this? A ride? "Yeah," I thought. "…on a school day?" I continued. I thought "oh yeah!"

At the beginning of the ride, I had no idea where we were headed or why we were going. I enjoyed riding in a car and was just happy to be riding around with my family. And, hey, missing a day from school didn't seem too bad either. Whenever we went on some sort of trip, I would try to hang my head out the window like a dog and take in the air in big gulps…this was no different. Mom harped, "Don't make me stop this car!" I knew what that meant, so I brought my head back inside of the car, but I began to let my arm flail in the air as if I was flying in an imaginary plane.

After about what seemed to be a couple of hours, we pulled up to a big building that looked like a hospital. It had a big playground area where I saw grownups dressed in white clothes and there were many kids around. Some of the kids were playing, but then some others were in wheelchairs and they only watched. I felt so bad for the kids in the wheelchairs and wondered what was wrong with them. I got sad. "Mom, what's this place?"

"We're in Norwich at a children's hospital," she replied.

Now of the four of us, Joey and I were the only 'children,' so I immediately began to wonder why we were stopping at this place…here at this creepy place that made me feel so sad. My mind was rushing and I was starting to wish that I were in school instead of being at this place. In school, even if I had to take another shot, eat spinach, or anything else, it would be better than looking at these sick kids. "Mom, I want to go home…now," I said. But, the look on her face told me that we would not be leaving yet.

We all got out of the car and walked inside this big building, it seemed so cold in there, not the kind of cold that you can feel on the outside, but the type that made you uneasy. I began to have a bad feeling. I started to get scared, but I knew my family was there with me, so I guess it was going to be okay. I tried to stay as close to Mom as possible. Being so close to her made me feel safe. "Go on over there and sit next to your brother," she said, "I need to talk to this lady for a minute."

Mom walked over to this big counter and talked to some other grownups. Joey, my father and I sat down and waited. I didn't remember anyone ever talking about this place so I didn't understand why we were here. It soon became clear to me that I was the reason for the stop. Mom was kneeling down, face to face with me trying to explain to me, a less than cooperative five-year old, why I was going to have to stay here in this hospital while they returned home. She said that I was sick and I needed to stay here to get better. "Sick? Me?" I thought. I didn't know what she was talking about because I felt good. "I want to go home with you!" It felt like I was being trapped in this place. Suddenly, it was hard for me to breathe and I started to shake badly. I kept trying to catch my breath in order to tell my mother I wanted to go home. Maybe she just didn't understand that I really wanted to go home! I became terrified just thinking that they were leaving me here alone. I had never been alone in my life. There had always been someone around me. My head pounded as thoughts ran through my young mind at the speed of sound. "How was this happening to me?" "Why can't I go home with the rest of my family?"

Home seemed like a million miles away from where I was. Words were pouring from my lips as fast as I could get them out. I remember pleading with Mom and Dad, "I'll be a good boy, I'll do whatever I'm 'spose to do." Right then, I tried to say whatever it took to go home. I told them I would not act up or hang my head, not even my arms, out the window anymore. I kept saying over and over again, "Please let me go home, I just want to go home." The pained look on Mom's face told me I wasn't going home. So, if reason wouldn't work, there's nothing like a good old-fashioned tantrum. I yelled and screamed while trying to run back to the car and begged my family to come quickly.

Soon, a nurse who looked larger than life came and took control of me and I watched my family walk away. How could they leave me here? I kept screaming as they walked away from me and I heard my mother tell Joey not to turn around. The nurse whisked me away for the start of an uncertain and scary time. I had never really been away from home and now I was in a place that seemed so foreign to me…it was so cold there, not the cold that you feel on the outside, it was chilling to the soul…it was uneasy.

One of those tests that they ran on me at school came back and said that I was not well. I later found out I had a disease called tuberculosis. Tuberculosis, ah to me, it was just a big word which meant I could not live at home anymore.

CHAPTER TWO
NEW BEGINNINGS

My first few days there were a blur. All of my thoughts focused on two things: why this happened, and how scared I felt in this faraway place. All the kids lived in an open bay area, and the beds were lined up down the full length of the room. This was nothing like my room at home. I didn't have any of my toys with me and didn't want to fight with the other kids to be able to play with the toys at the hospital. At my house, it was just Joey and I , but here there were kids everywhere. Now I spent my days sitting in a room with all these other kids. The grown-ups at the hospital taught us things like those that I learned in my school back home, but I didn't know these other kids and they didn't act like they wanted to know me. I just wanted to go home.

We would then have to eat whatever the nurses served. It was never something I liked…I have always been a picky eater. When I got scared or sad it was hard for me to eat, and I was both scared and sad, so I was not eating much at all. The nurses tried to make me eat more but I never seemed to be hungry.

It seemed like I was being poked and prodded every day for one thing or another. They would sometimes take me to a room and take x-rays. This room was always cold and the person taking the x-rays kept telling me to keep still, but it was hard to keep still in that cold room, especially when I had to place my chest against the x-ray machine. Sometimes I wondered what my family was doing but thoughts of home made me sad, so I tried to think of other things. In the beginning, I withdrew from everybody, but slowly started to open up to those around me.

The highlight of our week was all the kids gathering around the television on Sunday night to watch the Wonderful World of Disney. It seemed like that was the only time it was quiet there because all the kids loved to watch that show. My mother tried to visit every weekend; but this proved to be bittersweet. I was trying to adjust to my new environment and although I loved Mom and Joey, seeing them reminded me of a place that seemed a world away to me – they reminded me of home, they even smelled like home. "When can I come home?" I'd ask.

"When you get better, you'll be able to come home." I still didn't feel sick and Mom never said when that time would come. Then, there was the inevitable good-bye. That was always tough because seeing them leave felt like someone kicked me in the stomach. The first couple of times I tried to run out with them but the nurses always managed to grab me and take me back inside. After a while, when they'd leave, I started to act as if I didn't care. The problem was I really did. I guess I was beginning to form defense mechanisms, back then, some of which I still use today.

Through this time, I had developed a friendship with another kid who they also said was sick. His name was Timmy. He soon became my constant companion and playmate during my stay. It felt good to have someone with whom I could play and talk about anything. Now, even when Mom and Joey left from our visits it was okay because Timmy was there waiting to run around the playground with me. Strange, huh?

I remember the first day I saw the playground. I felt so sad for all of the sick kids then. But now I was having fun in the same place that made me feel sad at first. I would talk to some of the kids in wheelchairs and could not understand how they found a way to smile. How could the kids who could not walk find a way to laugh just like the rest of us? Strange, huh? Even though they said I was sick, I was happy that I could walk. If the children in the wheelchairs could laugh and smile then why couldn't I do the same? I knew that if I ever left this place, there was no way I would forget them because they found a way to be happy even though they may never walk.

It felt good to have someone like Timmy to be with; having a friend was the most important thing during this time. I knew that when I felt like crying, and many days I did, he would be there to put his arm around my shoulder. No matter how bad things got, I felt as long as Timmy was around that I'd be okay. While separated from my family, he became my family. Having someone close that cared about me was better than the medicine the nurses gave me every day. We made a pact to become brothers. You know how children do it; we'd spit in our hands and shake hands with the one who was your brother. Now I didn't have to long for Joey who was far away in Stamford, I had a brother close by. I knew as long as Timmy was there that I would be fine, but once again, change would alter the course of events and things would become turbulent...again.

One day something happened when we were outside playing on the merry-go-round. A couple of grown-ups arrived on the scene and motioned for Timmy to come over. He was very happy when he saw them and heard the news they told him. I never remember seeing him that happy before. Timmy then turned and looked at me with a faraway glance, waved, and left. That was the last time I ever saw him. Apparently, he got better and his parents came to take him home.

I just remember spinning on the merry-go-round feeling abandoned...again! The playground seemed to revert into that sad place I saw the first day. How can one place be a happy place one moment and a sad place the next? It was the same place yet it wasn't the same place. At that moment, I made up my mind that I would never allow anyone to get close to me ever again. Why?

People can only hurt you if they get close to you and there was no way this would happen again.

I totally withdrew from the other children. It was safer that way. My behavior made it clear to the staff that no matter what they did, I was keeping walls up to guard my feelings. One doctor did not give up and his persistence got the best of me. Sometimes, he would take me home with him and give me all the attention I craved, but I still didn't trust the doctor fully because I had already been betrayed before…twice: once by my family for leaving me in this wretched place and then by Timmy. We were buddies and if anyone should have known, Timmy should have known what I was going through. How could he leave me, too?

Soon after the time that the doctor tried to get me out of my shell, they said that I began to do better physically and was able to return home. I'd been away for about six months but in those six months, everyone I felt close to left me for some reason or another. How could I get over the feeling that eventually anyone I'd let close to me would find a reason to leave me? Can I risk it?

CHAPTER THREE
SOBERING REALITIES OF LIFE

Home. I made it back home to the small group that I thought I could count on to be there. It was just the four of us, me, my mother, everyone called her "Sugar," I just called her, "Mom," my brother Joey, who is two years older than I am, and my Dad, Rudy. Dad was in and out of the scene for most of my life, but he was there when I came home from the hospital so, I guess you could say I had a normal family existence…for a moment.

I had my share of boyhood pranks and adventures. Growing up in our house you quickly realized some harsh 'facts of life': there is no Santa Clause, Easter Bunny, and not everyone in the world is your friend. Money around our home was scarce and we learned how to live without many of life's luxuries. Reality can be a sobering thing and our world was chocked full of it.

For the better part of my formative years, it was my mother, my brother, and I. As the song says, "papa was a rolling stone" and he was out doing his thing in various parts of the country and even though my "Dad" was absent for most of my young life, he had a profound effect on me. His presence from time to time led to further confusion on my part but, like many women in that situation, Mom was strong and proud. She went to great lengths to be self-sufficient, and this was often times accomplished without any financial support from my father.

For a long while, we didn't own a car, so she would walk us to school every day and then she'd walk to work. After a long day at work, she'd then come home, prepare dinner and go to her other job. We wouldn't see her until the next morning when she would get us ready for school.

I can recall when Dad would show up from time to time. No matter how upset I felt about his absence, his brief presence would make things fine. My brother and I would get excited just at the prospect of seeing him, but it always seemed as if he was running late for some other commitment. He was just passing through. I would wonder why my mother was not as happy as we were to know that he was coming by, she always seemed troubled, but now I understand why. She hated to see us get our hopes up about doing things with him, only to see us eventually let down by his broken promises.

From time to time through the grapevine, we would get word on how Dad was doing and what he was doing. One particular time my dad came by and he had another woman and child with him. I couldn't understand how he could bring this other woman to our house and even more, how could he be with his new son and not want to be with my brother and I! I was probably about nine at this time and I became very angry and confused over all this, but Mom was solid and did her best to keep our family together: her, Joey and myself.

A proud and loving woman, I know my Mom was trying her best to put on a good face and provide the best for us while I imagined my Dad was living this great life with his great "other" family. This angered and frustrated me to no end. In my mind, he was living it up, no matter what his reality was. I began to develop a lingering hatred for my father. There were so many questions that I wanted him to answer: Why don't you love us? What did we do to cause you not to want to be a part of us…our family?

I was tired of having to make up stories about how my Dad was doing. I felt embarrassed and left out when we would have school events and I saw other kids there with their fathers. When people would ask me about my father, I began to tell them that he was dead. Well, to me he was dead. Besides, it was much easier to have a dead father than a father who was alive and didn't want to be around.

After a while, people soon stopped asking me questions and I was happy not to have to make excuses anymore. Seeing other kids have happy relationships with their fathers was extremely difficult. The sight of their joy drove a stake in my heart. "Was my Dad having this same joy with his other son?" Eventually I realized no matter how much I thought I hated my Dad; I only hated the fact that he wasn't there. I really longed for his acceptance in my life. Even though I tried to kill him in my mind, my heart would not let him die.

CHAPTER FOUR
DANGERS ALL AROUND

Other things happened when I was a child that helped me to understand the world can be a cold and dangerous place if I was not careful. Sometime during my first-grade year, I remember walking home from school with my brother and having a kid pull a gun on us. I didn't even know him; he just stood there pointing the gun at me and my friend. I was so afraid that I peed on myself; the kid thought it was really funny and started to laugh and taunt me. As much as that hurt my young old ego, it felt a lot better to at least be around to tell somebody what happened.

Back then, it was common to hear that somebody was shot or that somebody had a gun pulled on them. However, no matter how many stories I'd heard, it was scarier when it actually happened to me. I was never comfortable hearing those stories before that incident, nor afterwards. I guess a gun is just one of those things I'll never get used to. To this day, a gun still rattles me. I don't own one and don't think I ever will.

One day that same year, while walking home from school as I did any other day, I saw a bad school bus accident happen right in front of me. It was like slow motion when it happened. Another boy, around the same age as me, darted into the street without looking. The bus was coming down the street and didn't have time to come to a full stop. A moment before the impact the boy looked up, but it was too late. The bus was not traveling very fast at all, maybe 10 miles per hour, but the impact of a bus on a small child was devastating.

I just stood there on the corner for what seemed like forever hoping that he would get up. I said, "There is no way this is real!" to myself. I kept trying to think this was a movie or something but I realized this was real life when they put a white sheet over the kid as he lay in the street. I can remember walking home after that in a daze. I did not want to believe that in an instant a young boy was dead. I had heard about death, and seen people die on TV, but I had never seen anyone die in real life before. Many thoughts began to race through my mind as I continued to walk. Life was not supposed to be like this. What had that boy done to deserve to die so quickly? He was just a little kid like me, and little kids like us aren't supposed to die. Why would the God that everyone told me about take a little boy my age?

They told me that God protected the children, but this boy was not protected. He just died there in the middle of the street with no one around him, no family, and no friends to comfort him as he lay there. It was just the bus driver and I standing there. It just didn't seem right.

While all of those questions rolled through my mind, a wailing car horn shocked me back into reality. I'd aimlessly stepped into the path of oncoming traffic and one car almost ran into me. I didn't even notice that I'd been walking for about a mile and crossed into a busy intersection. The same God that moments ago took that little boy had just spared my life but for some reason I couldn't be happy. I thought, "Why was I fortunate but the other boy not so fortunate?" I had just done the same thing he did - not pay attention - but the result was very different.

For a long time after I saw that accident, it was difficult for me to walk home from school. I would sometimes take the long way home just so I would not have to walk past the spot where the little boy died. At other times, I would also remember the intersection where I was almost run over myself and would just wonder why I was still around. Before I could make sense of this, other things began to happen that would take up my attention.

One of the advantages of living by the Atlantic Ocean was being able to go to the beach for fun and games. We spent many afternoons riding our bikes down to the beach to hang out. Later the same year of the gun incident and tragic bus accident, a couple of my classmates went to the beach to play around. Back then, we would build makeshift rafts to float on the ocean.

The rafts were not very seaworthy, but when you're a kid, you sometimes take chances that unknowingly place you in dangerous situations. A Grace Jones song called "Scary but Fun" sums up much of our activities when we got bored as kids. We were only focused on the instant pleasure we were going to get from any activity, we never thought about the consequence of our actions. I don't even think we knew what consequences were!

Unfortunately, one day some of my classmates didn't think things through when they went rafting and eventually they were carried far from the shore by the undertow. In the wake of the swift, strong current, the poor workmanship of this group's raft became an issue. Eventually their vessel began to come apart and the four of them were in a battle for their lives. I didn't even know what an undertow was until we heard the story later. I thought to myself, "The grown-ups knew we went to the beach to play around; why didn't they tell us about the undertow before now?"

Far from shore, the four fourth graders debated the best course of action. The outcome of this debate would have profound effects on who lived and who died. There was a split on whether to try to swim back to the shore or ride it out. Both options were dangerous. To try to swim to shore was extremely risky due to the distance they had to cover, and there was no guarantee the coast guard would spot them if they stayed on the raft. In the end, two decided to swim and the other two would ride it out in hopes that someone would spot and rescue them.

The two who decided to swim for it never considered the undertow and quickly found themselves in a more desperate predicament. They attempted to make it back to the raft but the unforgiving current and fatigue were too much for their bodies to overcome. When people were telling us the story, I began to feel a tremendous sense of loss.

Can you imagine watching a couple of your friends drowning right in front of you? At seeing this, terror and panic engulfed the two who remained on a vessel, which was becoming less seaworthy by the moment. As darkness began to replace light, the little boys' hopes faded as quickly as the day. Fear gripped the two cold and scared boys. The type of fear that sends chills down your back. I got those same chills just listening to the story.

I imagine that they wondered if this was how their lives would end or if someone would save them. The raft continued drifting further and further from the shore and all that represented safety was becoming unreachable. Before compounding the day's tragedy, just when all seemed lost, the Coast Guard spotted them drifting out to sea and managed to rescue the remaining two boys. Four went out: two returned to shore, and two are now with God. No one that we knew ever went rafting again after that.

I remember going back to school and hearing the teacher talk about it, I felt so bad for a classmate of mine because she lost her brother. I could remember what it's like to feel left and alone from my days in the hospital but my classmate was not going to get her brother Michael back, there would never be a reunion for her. At least I had that; I was starting to understand things could always be worse. She was so sad. There was nothing we could do to cheer her up, and that made me feel helpless.

DREAMS OF DEATH

Seeing and hearing about all these people around me, dying began to get to me. During this period of my fear of death, my brother was there for me. I would be hysterical in my fear of what death held for me I remember lying in my bed and being terrified about going to sleep because I was afraid of dying. I would cry and between sobs say "I don't wanna die! I don't wanna die!" Joey would try to comfort me; he'd say that I didn't need to be afraid of anything. Inside, I felt like if he had seen what I had seen, he'd be scared, too.

Thoughts of a dark and scary place dominated my dreams, a place where there would be nothing but loneliness and despair. I could hear the screams of those who had died before me. They cried out in the darkness for comfort and hope, but there was no comfort for them and hope was lost. I just kept thinking about not waking up ever again. Not being able to see Mom and Joey again was a punishment I didn't want. I wondered why I had to die at all – why did anyone have to die. I guess all of these issues and questions were just too much for my immature mind to handle, so I was just terrified and sad.

This went on every night for months and months. I would sometimes just want to lie in my mother's bed because it was the only place that I felt safe. No matter how scared I was, I knew that she would make me feel better. Sometimes she sang lullabies to me before I'd fall asleep. She would then carry me to my bed for the night. She always gave me comforting hugs when I was having one of my nightmares. No matter how tired she was, she found a way to provide security and warmth. She always knew what I needed and seemed to possess an endless supply of love.

I must admit that Joey showed a great deal of patience and love in helping me through this period in my life. Mom and Joey helped me understand hope and for that, I will always be grateful. But as I stated earlier the fourth grade for me was a very turbulent year.

In addition to all that which took place, there was also this pervert in our community who was walking around cutting off little boys' penises. On top of everything else, there was now another reason for me to dread the walk home from school. For our safety, we walked home in packs. Talk of this person who was hurting kids was all around. The more I heard of him, the worse I felt. What kind of person would do something so crazy to little boys? So, while many kids were focusing on the things kids think about, like Santa Clause or the Easter bunny, the kids in my neighborhood dealt with a full-blown case of reality.

Mom gave us stern lectures about being careful when outside. She always put us first and worried a great deal about us when we left the house. Our community really came together during this time. When we walked home from school, the adults in the neighborhood kept a close eye on us, even if they did not know us. Eventually, we stopped hearing about kids being hurt from this guy. I'm not sure if they caught him or he just moved on, all I knew was that I felt better.

CHAPTER FIVE
TEACHING A MAN TO BE A MAN

To improve on the past, it is important that you first understand the past. Relationships and structure are keys to developing young men and women for the future. The fact that my Dad wasn't a positive male role model for Joey and I still has effects on both of us. We missed many conversations with him, learning opportunities that we lost and "father – son" experiences we never shared. Although my father was not there during most of my early years, several key figures stepped in as positive male influences during my lifetime.

UNCLE AARON

Aaron is my father's brother. Because of my Dad's 'in today, out today' interaction, I think Uncle Aaron felt a bit obligated to help us. When I was around 10 yrs. old, I began to work at the cleaners he owned. I cleaned around the business and put cardboard guards on hangers. I think it was a way for him to keep his eye on me after school…also it was a good way for him to get some slave labor. My salary was $5.00 a week and he ended up owing me $75.00. I guess the moral of the story is not to work for relatives…without a contract.

Uncle Aaron was and is one of the most giving men I have ever met. His generosity is the main reason he never really made it as a businessman. If there was a need, he would help first, and then he figured out later how he could cover for it. Not too many people would just give without concern about when or if you could repay them. I saw him do that repeatedly…he did it for others but mostly, he did it for us.

I never wanted to miss being outside playing with my friends, but Uncle Aaron wouldn't let me miss being at work either, so I had to figure out a way to do both. I worked out a deal with Uncle Aaron so that I could come in late because I wanted to play football with my friends. He was cool like that and man, I was so excited because I loved football. Excited about my deal, the next day I got up and couldn't think of anything else but being able to play in that game. I looked in the refrigerator at home, didn't see anything I wanted to eat so I didn't eat. This day was particularly hot, but playing football with my friends was my number one priority.

The football game was going great and we were winning, things could not have been better. Suddenly I began to feel queasy and sweat began to pour off me. I sat down to try to regroup but then the world seemed like it was spinning around. I guess I must have blacked out and when I came to, Uncle Aaron was there picking me up and carrying me to his car. We rode for what seemed forever. It was only a couple of miles but when you're ill, time seems to drag. He rushed me into the hospital and soon a doctor came and began to examine me. The doctor quickly determined I was severely dehydrated and began to ask me questions.

"What have you eaten today?"

"There was nothing to eat at my house." I replied.

Uncle Aaron exploded out of his chair and said, "Boy what are you talking about? You know there's food at your house!" Well, in my mind, since there was nothing at my house that I wanted to eat, there was nothing to eat. Motioning to Uncle Aaron to calm down, the doctor continued to probe.

"What were you doing when you became ill?" "I was just playing with my friends but was getting ready to go to my job."

"Surely, you're too young to have a job," the doctor said.

"Oh yes I do." I boasted. "I work for my uncle at his cleaners."

Man, just then, the look on Uncle Aaron's face told me that if he could have choked me and gotten away with it that he would have. I believe the doctor was ready to call the child welfare agency or something. He must have thought my Uncle was starving me and working me to death. It took a lot of fast-talking from Uncle Aaron before the doctor understood that there was food at our house and that my job was just a way to keep an eye on me. When Mom heard this story, she just shook her head and said, "That son of mine will always keep things interesting." Later we all laughed about my delirious ramblings, but it was years later.

By the age of 13, I was running the lottery machine and collecting money for him. He trusted me and I felt good about earning his trust. He also gave me rewards for having good grades in school. I was a good student anyway and I really didn't need the incentive to do well. I just wanted to please Mom and Uncle Aaron. He would take me to basketball games when I played across town and whatever I needed, he made sure I had it. Even when I was afraid that I would not be able to play basketball because I didn't have the money to buy my uniform, Uncle Aaron was there. Times were tough back then, we were barely making it, but Uncle Aaron always seemed to smooth things out for us.

During the summers, Uncle Aaron would make a big production about taking Joey and me to North Carolina. He said that it was to expose us to our "roots." So, he brought us back to our birthplace, introduced us to people and experiences we didn't know or wouldn't have growing up in Connecticut. Uncle Aaron was big on stressing the history of our family and trying to provide a sense of tradition, so we looked forward to our trips to the south. On these trips, he also taught me how to play cards for money…and that is how I ended up winning from him all of the money he should have paid me. There's more than one way to skin a cat! We never talked about my Dad, but I felt he knew it ate at me and he tried to fill the gap. He took on the role of disciplinarian in my life, too. Ooooh, weeee, I remember one of the worst beatings I ever got came at his hand. He had taken Joey and I down to a family gathering in North Carolina. We left from my aunt's house to go to another location for a visit. Now, I was notorious for sleeping in cars, so they woke me up after we arrived at the new location. We were there for a long while; I got up and told my brother I wanted to go back to my aunt's house. Being the smart-aleck, big brother he was, Joey said, "Well, then just go to the corner and make a left and keep walking until you see Aunt Margaret's house."

Remember, I slept the whole ride over so I had no idea how far out we were from Aunt Margaret's or if we were even in the same town. Undaunted by his sarcasm, I began to walk. Sometime into my journey, I recall thinking, "Why is it taking me so long to get back to Auntie's house?"

About 15 minutes later, my uncle pulled up alongside me and asked, "Where the heck you think you going, boy?" Before I could explain or say anything at all, he was out of the car and on me like a cheap suit in a rainstorm. It seems my calculations were a little off. I guess I slept longer than I thought because we were about 30 miles from Auntie's house and at the rate I was walking, it would take me a week to get there. To this day, he never lets me forget he had to "put it on me," as he likes to say.

Uncle Aaron had a profound influence on my life and the man I am is only a reflection of the love and patience he freely gave us. Through his example, I started to believe some things are free and precious. As I reminisce on my relationship with Uncle Aaron, many things come to mind, but even though Uncle Aaron was there, he was not my father and the gnawing questions surrounding Dad's absence haunted me.

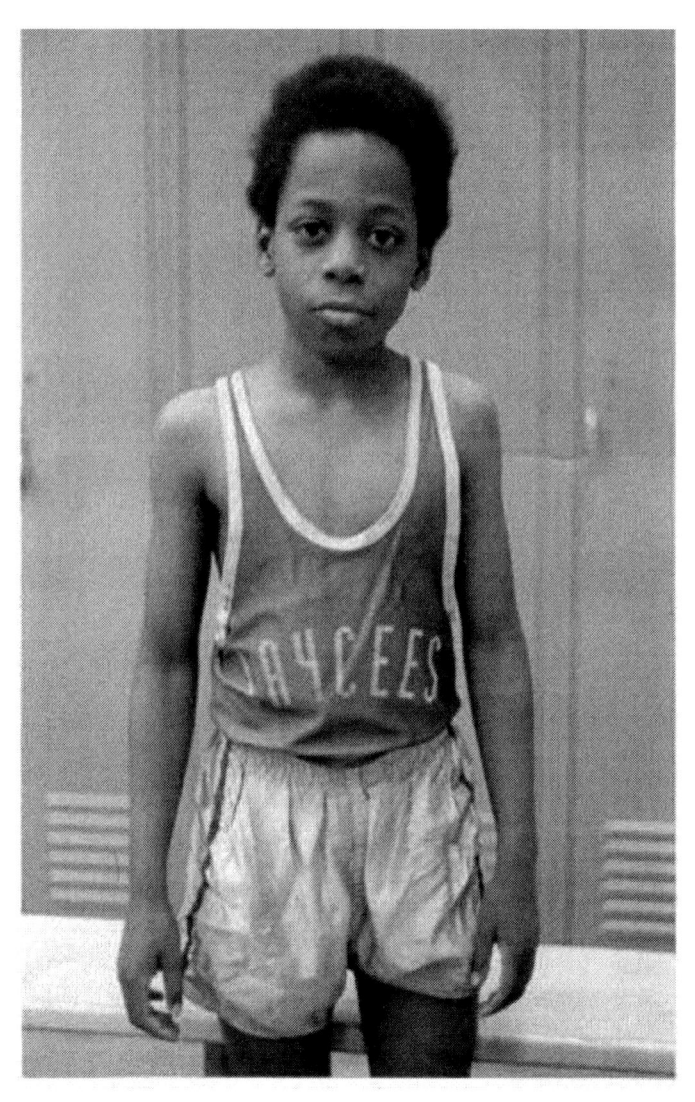

Big Ballin'

CHAPTER SIX
BEGGING MOM

After many years of my Dad coming in and out of our lives, Joey and I started to put pressure on my mother to get back with him. I could tell she was not enthusiastic about our suggestion; my father had a history of carousing…a family trait, as I would later find out. Eventually, she allowed him back into the house and we were a nuclear family again. Wow, I would finally be able to do and share things with my father. We were back in stride, taking the family portraits, him double-checking our homework, reviewing our grades and going with us to family gatherings. He would even take me out back and shoot hoops on a makeshift goal.

One of the things I really enjoyed was playing a game called Strikeout – a simulated baseball game that only required two players. There was no running at all. One pitched and one swung at the ball. In Strikeout, the pitcher had to send the ball to a strike zone that was a square box painted on the side of a building. How far you hit the ball determined your place on the base pads. In the city, we came up with creative ways to play games because there weren't any baseball diamonds near our house.

Sports was one of my father's passions, I mentioned one of the others earlier. I often felt like he was more or less reminiscing about his past when we played and even wondered if he even knew I was there. Somebody told me that Dad once was a very good baseball player and he could have been in the major leagues if he had stayed with it. It never dawned on me that some of Dad's reactions were born out of his unfulfilled dreams. Hmmm?

Time has a way of revealing things to us eventually and I realized my relationship with my father lacked substance and depth. When I would try to ask him questions regarding anything on an emotional level, he would just change the subject. As my body began to change, there were questions needing answers and some things a boy doesn't feel comfortable discussing with his mother. I can think back to a time when I tried to discuss the subject of girls with my father, I was a teenager then, and he quickly said, "Why are you talking to me about things like this?"

I cannot recall as a child or even as young adult ever seeing my father express any type of emotion towards me, well not any other than anger. This was one of the reasons he could not comfortably discuss matters of the heart with anyone, not with us, not with Mom either. It's difficult to talk about things you that you are suppressing. His generation overwhelmingly believed men did not cry or show feelings. I didn't realize that he was teaching me some of those same lessons. Although, I like to say that I can control it now, I believe I inherited this trait, this lack of communication, from Dad; And, it prevailed during many of my adolescent relationships and experiences.

To see a man uninhibited emotionally was rare and refreshing. On some levels, it made other men around him insecure. No real man wanted to be associated with someone perceived as soft, and everybody labeled any man who was open emotionally as "soft." It takes a real man to be able to overcome the stigma and negative stereotype of being open with his feelings. We'd immediately label such a guy as a punk, a sissy, or even worse. That sure wasn't Dad, but I am glad that there was one man in my life I can recall who had no problem with displaying his inner self.

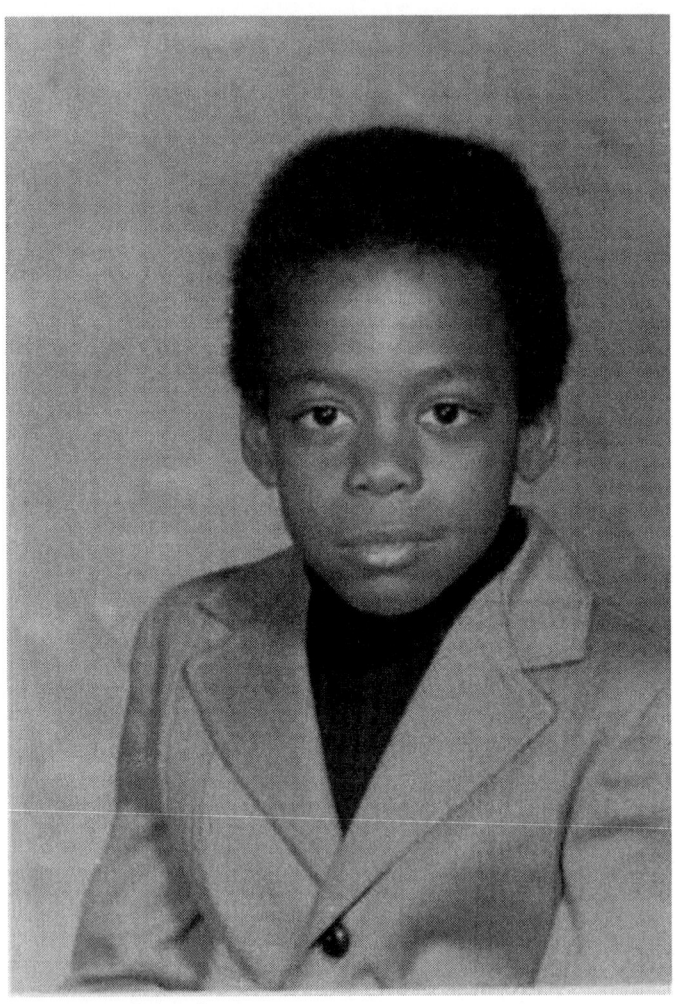

Elementary School

CHAPTER SEVEN
A MAN AIN'T SUPPOSED TO CRY

Uncle Robert, Dad's other brother, was an incredibly sensitive and caring individual. His personality, his warmth, and presence balanced the harshness of Dad's rigidity. I can't recall ever seeing Uncle Robert alone. He always had someone around him; and was a well-liked person and maybe it was because he was so caring. No matter how engaged he was in a conversation, Uncle Robert would stop what he was doing and acknowledge me. Not only would he acknowledge my presence, but he also made a point of telling whoever he was with how proud he was that I was his nephew. I thought, "How could he be so proud of me, I hadn't done anything for him." After hearing him say this a few times, the question began to eat at me. No one ever complimented me unless I had done something for them, yet Uncle Robert encouraged me every chance he had.

Again, unlike Dad, Uncle Robert always made it a point to hug and kiss me whenever he saw me, and it didn't matter where we were at the time. I remember once in the fourth grade; he came to school to visit my cousin Darrin and I saw him coming. Well, I knew what I was in for so I tried to avoid him; but, too late, he noticed me and made a "beeline" my way. Right there, in front of my entire class, Uncle Robert laid a wet kiss on my cheek…ooooh how embarrassing.

The whole class began to laugh and tease me about the incident. I now realize that even at a young age I was already uncomfortable with receiving open love or giving it in return. Uncle Robert knew that I did not feel comfortable with his expression of love in the form of a kiss, but that did not bother him. I guess his mind was made up; he would openly express himself to me no matter what.

One day I ran into him in the neighborhood, and this was the first time I can recall running into him when he was alone. As we sat together in a park near home, I saw this as my chance to get my questions answered.

"Uncle Robert..." I started.

"Yeah Anthony"

"...why you always saying you proud of me?"

He smiled a little and told me that the best things in life were free and he learned to value all of the things given to him. Uncle Robert viewed each of us in our family as a gift to cherish. He said, "You never have to do anything for me to be proud of you but be yourself." He asked me to close my eyes and listen. He then asked, "What do you hear?"

I never concentrated to listen so hard in my life. I heard leaves rustling as the wind blew, birds chirping, and people playing. He said "The same God that created the wind to blow the leaves, made the birds to sing, and allows the people to play created you." Uncle Robert said, "If you look, you can always see God."

Uncle Robert enjoyed looking at the world. That day he helped me see many things. I understood why he was proud of those he loved and why he always needed to show his love for us with those hugs and kisses. Uncle Robert said no matter what the situation was, with God, there was always hope. He chose not to focus on what everyone else saw with their eyes, instead he tried looking at things the way God who created them would see them. He understood that love is love, whether it is returned or not. It isn't based on the reaction of the one receiving love; it is more concerned with the one who gives love.

I remember seeing Uncle Robert shortly before he passed away and instead of worrying about himself, his first thoughts were of his family. Even though he appeared to be in much pain, he did not complain or allow me to focus on his condition; instead, his thoughts were about the success of those left after him. As I talked to him in the hospital, I realized that I was in the presence of the most loving person I had ever met. His love caused his present pain and suffering to become irrelevant when compared to passing his message of hope and promise to me.

He understood the gift of each moment and did not allow anything to distract him from his message to me. He told me he loved me, and I believed it, and knew that if anyone knew what love meant it was Uncle Robert. When I embraced him before I left his room, I knew deep inside that it was the last time that I would see him alive again and I remember feeling helpless. I made sure to get close to his face because I needed one more kiss from him.

How could a person going through so much find it in their spirit to place others before himself? I searched for the words to say, words that would encourage him. Yet, it was Uncle Robert offering the encouragement, the strength, and comfort to me. We hugged, and I secretly prayed that during that embrace I'd receive his spirit of love to share with others.

"I need for you to take care of yourself, and don't worry about me because it was going to be fine," he said. He quietly taught me the lesson of love's courage through his life. He understood that love reaches out even when those we love pull away. He taught that love doesn't allow pain and rejection to stop it from embracing. He taught that love is not confined to societal norms or expectation. Love just is and it does what it wishes because no one can contain love and Uncle Robert was love in the truest sense. I would hope that I carry a piece of his sensitivity and genuine touch with me. There are times, like right now; I would kill for just one kiss from him. Rest well Uncle Robert.

CHAPTER EIGHT
RUNNING WITH THE PACK

Somehow, I managed to navigate through the wild, wild days of my adolescence. I went through a lot of tough times but only with the help of a couple of true friends. Although my brother was always there for me, it was their friendships that helped me grow from an isolated, withdrawn child to an animated, outgoing young man. In great measure, I learned about life, loyalty, and commitment through my friendships with Cuda and Jake. Through thick and thin, I could always count on these two fellas.

CUDA

I met Cuda in the fourth grade and we naturally hit it off. He is Haitian and speaks French fluently and I am sure that fascinated me. As children, we mocked anything we didn't understand, the word out on Cuda was that he would not respond back to teasing. Since none of us spoke French, Cuda was an obvious target.

My neighborhood was rough on you if you had something we perceived as strange or a weakness. Hey, we were children. We didn't have a clue that the very reason we teased him about was the very thing that made him outstanding and special. Heck, none of us had a clue that a 'second' language would mean so much when we got older? Even though I was his friend, subtly, I joined in with the rest of the kids and did my fair share of teasing, too. Well, to tell the truth, in many cases, I was the instigator.

Cuda never got angry at my teasing and strangely enough, we became the best of friends. At the age of nine, Cuda had the personality, character, and confidence that many of us don't grow into until we are much older and, in some ways, I longed to be like that. We were almost inseparable. Either I was at his house or he was at mine. We just naturally belonged together like hamburger and French fries – it's hard to imagine one without the other. I became a part of his family and he sure became a part of mine.

Cuda was always tinkering on something. He had skills to use hands to fix whatever needed fixing. One time, Mom bought me a bike; it may as well have been for the both of us because I let Cuda use it whenever he wanted. See, that's what partners do for each other. I really think that he used my bike as a pattern because before long, he found different parts and built a bike of his own. That tripped me out! Now, I mean, I was all thumbs, whenever I got a flat or my chain popped off, I had to get Cuda to fix it. When my bike began to break down too much, he built me one, and it worked like a charm. After a while, I forgot that it wasn't the one Mom bought from the store – I couldn't tell the difference.

We went to the same schools, even had the same classes for five years. We were notorious for pulling foolish pranks. Sometimes we'd open a carton of milk, creep up to a classroom, open the door, and then throw the milk into the class. Other times, we'd try to cop a feel from a girl and try to blame someone else. I was good at that one. For the most part, I was very afraid of girls and copping a feel was the closest I thought I would ever get to doing anything with them. We had a lot of good times in school, until the ninth grade when Cuda decided he wanted to become a chef. So, he went to a trade school and I went to a regular high school.

JAKE

Although Cuda and I go way back, it wasn't until the first day of high school that I met the third part of our trio, Jake Maye. While in the gym for freshman orientation, he came up to me and said "Are you sure you're in the right place?" You see, I was very small for my age and he thought I was supposed to be in junior high or elementary school. Now, I can tell you that our first encounter didn't do much to boost my confidence in this strange new world, but we immediately bonded and forged a friendship that would only grow stronger.

The thing I admired about Jake was that he always knew what he wanted out of life and led a focused and energetic pursuit towards his goals. Jake was very conscientious when it came to schoolwork and working odd jobs. He would take part of his income and help pay the bills around his house. Although his living conditions weren't the best, he had a loving family environment. The way he carried himself made him seem out of place around our neighborhood. While most of the people we knew focused on superficial things, Jake always looked beyond his circumstances to reach for new horizons. Even in the 9th grade, he knew he wanted to be a lawyer and provide for his family. I didn't know of anyone who left the projects and became a lawyer.

In the midst of the madness around him, Jake seemed immune from many of the challenges facing many of the boys our age and from our poor neighborhood. He seized every opportunity presented to him. He did not wait for someone to give him something, he did what it took to get whatever he wanted, whether it was by doing his homework or by exploiting every program designed to benefit him, Jake just made things work for him.

Another funny thing about him was how polished and well-spoken he was and it made him stick out like a sore thumb. A lot of kids running around in our neighborhood expressed themselves with foul language and aggressive tones, but Jake was soft spoken and had a great command of the English language. He seemed like a man going for a stroll in a park when you saw him, oblivious to the subtle or the overt distractions the world provided. Others guys in the neighborhood began to take notice of Jake's focus and mocked him unmercifully.

"You trying to sound like a white boy!" they'd say.

Sometimes he'd yell back, "How is a black person supposed to speak?" But more often than not, he'd just shake his head and continue with the task at hand. After a while, the others stopped taunting him and some of them even started encouraging him.

THE CREW

Well, it was the three of us; determined, stubborn and at times, well, most of the time, just plain 'ole crazy. With the courage I gained from having Cuda and Jake to back me up in anything, I eventually mustered up the nerve to ask a girl for her number. Man, after that, things began to get more interesting. Ooooh wee, Monica Brown, mmm, mmm, mmm. I sure didn't know what to do, but with my boys, we could figure out anything. Monica and I talked on the phone a couple of times. After only a few conversations, I swear it was my smooth rap that convinced her to invite me to her house. I just knew that she would be the first girl I would ever kiss, but I wondered why she was so at ease about asking me over when I was totally petrified. I didn't know anything about what to do around a girl. So, you know I had to turn to my boys!

Of the three of us, Cuda was the only one seriously into someone. Surely, he knew how to kiss because he had been involved with Cindy. As for Jake, well I wasn't sure about his prowess, because he seemed even more confused and scared about girls than I was. Jake was the kind of guy who would get excited when other guys would talk about the girls they were dating. He'd always say, "So, what happened next?!" when someone was telling their story. We all thought that if he didn't get a girl soon that he would go crazy.

Now Monica lived a couple of miles away from me and up until now, I would walk to her house and babble about nothing because I did not know what else to do. I heard other guys talking about kissing and things, but I couldn't ask them how to do it because, surely, I'd lose major cool points. The fellas knew I had a girlfriend so I guess they assumed I knew what I was doing. They were wrong, because even though several weeks passed, the only thing happening between Monica and I was a bunch of small talk. But she kept insisting that I walk her all the way to her house and most of the time we'd get there at a time when her mother wouldn't be there – any fool could tell that she wanted it bad. What's a brotha to do?

I didn't have any practical experiences doing what I knew we were going to do, so watching the soap operas gave me some insight on how to hold my head if I ever was put in a position to kiss a girl. For days, I watched how the actors would do it on TV. I played the picture over and over in my mind trying to ensure that I modeled my actions after them…after all; they were getting all of the action.

I could tell that Monica was getting tired of my routine, but I didn't know what else to do. One day the unthinkable happened; I ran out of small talk and it was very awkward. Before I knew what happened she laid her lips on mine and all I could do was to try to go with the flow. Do I keep my eyes open? What do I do with my hands? Why in the world am I drooling? These few questions thundered through my mind. You know I forgot all of the lessons I learned from the actors on the soap operas, so I just hung on for dear life and prayed that she didn't know enough as to know that I didn't know anything at all.

I wish I could write that I came off like a natural but that wouldn't be correct. I was 13 at the time and for the entire summer we practiced kissing, I got pretty good at it too, but I didn't want to press my luck trying to go any further. There was huge pressure from some of the fellas to go all the way with a girl. I wondered if I really wanted to kiss her or did, I just want to build up my street credibility. Monica and I ended up going to different high schools and that was the end of that but I had my stories to brag about to the fellas for a long time.

CHAPTER NINE
GROWING PAINS

High school was a time of confusion and exploration. Easily, my most traumatic period was my freshman year. I did not know what I wanted to do in my future so I had no appreciation for what an education could offer me. It's as the Bible says, "Where there is no vision the people perish." I was an independent thinker for the most part, but not having any focus made me susceptible for whatever passing idea that anybody presented.

My body was starting to act in ways it had never done before. My voice was cracking at the least opportune time and I started to grow hair in places where none had previously existed. Although the most embarrassing phenomenon I experienced was getting unannounced boners. Once my mother walked into the room and I was in the midst of experiencing an unexpected salute. I was speechless and when I finally tried to respond my voice let me down again by cracking. I believe my mother chuckled under her breath as she left the room. I had a full-blown case of puberty.

My lack of focus coupled with the major physical changes was the prime ingredients for a tumultuous year. The initial days at Rippowam High School were intimidating for more reasons than being in a new school. The upperclassmen had a practice called initiation where they pummeled the freshmen whenever they could catch one. I witnessed many of my partners get pounded unmercifully in bathrooms and on the bus going home from school.

The bus was the most intimidating part because everyone had to catch the bus home. Inevitably, on the way home the upperclassmen would get up and say it's time to break in a couple of freshmen. They would grab whomever they wanted to, bring them to the back of the bus, and commence to opening a can of whoop ass. The freshman would look at the bus driver in hopes that they would restore order. To date, I'm not aware of any bus driver intervention to stop one of these bashings.

They just continued to look forward and drive the bus as the pained yelps of poor freshman provided a serenade for the ride home. Freshmen really didn't stick together well during this; it was every man for himself. I can remember a couple of occasions where I continued to run and tried to ignore the screams of one of my partners, maybe I was being groomed to be a bus driver.

The beatings really got out of hand sometimes, some folks were thrown down stairs, and it was common to hear about someone sustaining broken bones. It seemed like the upperclassmen took greater pleasure in breaking down the bigger freshmen. You would see the bigger ones try to put up a good fight but it was a matter of numbers. It didn't matter how big you were because you were attacked in waves.

The thing that always got me was some guys who you thought were hard and then you'd see them crying like a baby after a few blows. I made up my mind that no matter what happened, I was not going to break down; fortunately, the level of abuse I had to endure was not too great. I had found favor with some of the toughest upperclassmen at Rippowam. They told me that if anyone touched me to let them know and they'd even the score so I didn't have too bad a time of it.

Some of the freshmen made it hard on themselves even before the school year started. Old heads warned me to keep cool and not to make waves with any upperclassmen before the school year started. But some of my friends didn't follow that advice. They seemed to think it was a big joke when guys would say what was going to happen when school started. They would even start selling "woof tickets" to these guys, you know running their mouths about how they weren't concerned about initiation, and they woofed on and on about how no one would lay a hand on them. BIG MISTAKE! They were the first ones on the hit list and they would soon regret their bravado.

The initiation period lasted about three weeks. If you hung in there or hadn't changed schools by then, they left you alone. Some guys actually left and went to other schools because they couldn't deal with it. For the record Jake hung in there and on one occasion I witnessed how durable he was as he took a thrashing at the hand of a couple of fellas. I wanted to help but fear got the best of me. He didn't see me and neither did his assailants, so I just tipped away to safety. As for Cuda, well let's just say they don't do that sort of stuff in trade schools; my guess is while Jake and I were running for our lives, Cuda was baking cakes.

BUT WHEN I BECAME A MAN…

PHASE II

CHAPTER TEN
WELCOME TO THE REAL WORLD

Once the ordeal of a daily pounding was over, we all tried to regroup and assume a normal existence. A couple of schools were closer to where we lived than Rippowam, but there was a push for more diversity, so the kids in my neighborhood had to ride the bus across town. In a matter of a few days, I realized this concept would place me in a situation where I would have to face some things that were unpleasant.

Our high school was about 80% Caucasian and 20% minority and most of us there would speak and act out on our thoughts and beliefs without thinking of the consequences for our actions. As you grow older, you learn to choose your words more carefully and to think before you act, but not when you are 13, 15, or even 17. The impulsive actions of groups of these teenagers soon brought me face to face with a portion of the 80% who let me know they did not welcome any of the 20% that had invaded their grounds. Although I must add, many of the students did welcome us, and I actually became friends with a few.

Many of the school's restroom walls were covered with graffiti declaring the hatred that provided an undercurrent at Rippowam. And between classes, there was an onslaught of racial slurs hurled at us, which we returned, when we walked to class. When we were in gym, it seemed like I was always the one who was picked on by groups of white kids. If I was them, I'd come after me, too because I was the smallest kid in the class.

We had a typical gym teacher, Coach Jemison. He was an old sports enthusiast whose best days were way past him. He loved the physicality of contact sports. When we played indoor soccer, he encouraged us to smash each other into the walls and bleachers. Coach Jemison was always the first to comment on a good check when you got the ball from someone and I must admit I started to enjoy the rush I got from slamming into someone. When things got to a boiling point, Coach Jemison was always there to diffuse the situation.

Eventually, for me, this undercurrent of racial friction came to a boiling point when I had a heated exchange with a group of white students. I disliked them because they were different, and I knew they didn't like me, so it didn't matter. I told my friends that the next time any one of them gave me some lip, I was going to give them something they'd remember. I didn't have to wait long.

There was this one kid named Brad who hated blacks and made a point of letting anyone who'd listen know it. One day, we were in science class together and he was into his usual routine of trying to flex on everyone in the class because he was the biggest kid in class. Brad seemed to have a mean streak and welcomed any opportunity to display his hatred for others around him. The teacher never said anything either, he just let him run the class. He was probably just happy because he had Brad around to keep the class in fear or the teacher shared many of Brad's same views but couldn't say anything. Well, I made up my mind that I wasn't going to take anymore from him and neither of them counted on the fact that one little squirt like me would say, "Enough is enough."

So, this time as Brad came around with his routine of calling us niggers, I simply said something to remind him that his birth was the result of his mother's involvement with various farm animals. I don't remember my exact words but he didn't take them very well and before I knew it, I was kicked out of class. Day after day, everyone heard Brad repeatedly call us niggers, but he never received any punishment. One comment and I got detention. Why?!

The next day, Brad went around the school telling everyone that when he saw me that I was going to eat my words along with my teeth. The thing that really got me was he was woofing to my boys and they didn't do or say anything! Again, I had to wrestle with the fight or flight dilemma. Running from the upperclassmen during initiation was one thing but this was different. Initiation was wrong, but at least I understood it. We got beat up for no reason other than being freshmen but bigotry was personal. It was different because he singled me out because of my heritage.

I was just as afraid of Brad as I was of the upperclassmen, but there was no way I was going to run. This was a one-man operation. Jake and a couple others, who knew about the situation, began to tell me of what Brad intended to do to me. I wanted to ask them to help me. Nah, I couldn't do it, something inside would not let me. This was one of those times when I had to walk alone.

The next day I was on my way to class, I saw Brad coming, and I got nervous. I was more afraid of him than the guys who chased me around during initiation. At least the guys who pounded you during initiation didn't hate you, this was very different, and this was for keeps. Brad walked up to me and said "Now what are you going to do, nigger?" To be honest, I didn't know, but it was on.

I had heard the word nigger more times than I wanted to remember. But there was something particularly vexing about the way he said it. His words, laced with venom, touched my very core and I began to feel what he spewed: hatred. The students in the hallway encircled the two of us, and there was no way of retreat available. I was not looking for one. I wanted a piece of him. Boiling aggression replaced any fear I had. I quickly sized up the situation: he was well over six feet tall; I was barely five feet tall; he had long arms and

I would have to get too close to him to have any chance. There was no backing down now.

Before I knew what happened he knocked my books from my hands and out of the corner of my eye, I could see our science teacher watching; I briefly detected a slight grin on his face. My guess is that his money was on Brad and the way things looked, I thought that was a pretty good bet. Why was my teacher letting this happen? Unfortunately, there was not time to ponder this question; there were more pressing matters at hand. Once my books hit the ground, I went at Brad with all I had. He took a good swing at me while I was trying to get inside at him. I knew that if I had any chance, I'd have to be willing to take some punishment because I had to get close to him to do my damage.

His fist caught the side of my head and momentarily stunned me but I focused on my target; his rib cage was an inviting location for my focus. This strategy was born from a game my brother played with me called "going to the ropes." In this game, I would stand against a wall and my brother and I would exchange body shots. The only way I could come away from the wall was to fight my way out. This was Joey's way of helping me to become tough. My brother would say "Kill the body and the head will die." I sure hoped he was right because this was the strategy I planned to use on Brad. I weathered Brad's first blow to my head, but when I saw him swinging again, I managed to avoid the second blow and bear down on his ribs. I bit down on my lip and was determined to finish what he'd started. Leading with my shoulder, I managed to get to inside his comfort zone with a football type charge. Once there, I drove my shoulder into his ribs and backed him into the wall lockers. As we hit the lockers, I could hear the air escape from his body. Now, I had him cornered and I did not intend to let him out. He would have to fight his way out of the corner.

I don't think he had ever gone to the ropes before. A couple of well-placed body shots accomplished their intended purpose and Brad buckled at the knees. From there I managed to knock him on the ground. There is no height advantage on the ground and I was at home rolling on the floor. My brief time on the wrestling team would now pay an unexpected dividend.

In the background, I could hear all the other students yelling at the sight of our grappling. I managed to get on top of him and all he could do was try to deflect the barrage of blows I rained upon his head. A couple of punches got through clean and I could tell I had taken the heart out of him. All I could think about was all the abuse he had heaped upon me and I felt rage welling up in me. "How does it feel to get pounded by a nigger?" I asked over and over, feeling a rage that even shook me.

For a moment, I was someone else; a person filled with rage caring about nothing except hurting someone. My science teacher came out and pulled me off of him. How quickly would his intervention had been if I'd been on the bottom? I was suspended and my mother was very understanding once I explained what happened. I never had any more trouble out of Brad or anyone else for that matter…to be honest that's all I really wanted.

As much as I hated Brad during this situation, something troubled me more. For a moment, I became the thing that I hated. In my heart, I became just as cruel and bitter as he was to me. There was a moment I wanted to hurt him badly. I wasn't focused on self-defense, rather fixated on rendering pain and suffering. Upon further reflection I realized then that the truth was that we must change the world and not let the world change us. I couldn't take on Brad's hatred and anger, so I left it right there in the hallways of Rippowam High School.

CHAPTER ELEVEN
GIRLS, GIRLS, GIRLS

Once we got to the age when we began to notice girls, our entire world turned upside down. Oh, it was over when we no longer saw girls as people to play childhood games with or chase them around with small lizards, frogs or any other yucky thing we could find. But soon we noticed the distinct differences between them and us. We were curious and attracted both at the same time. It was a confusing and awkward time for us. This was one of those things I dare not ask my Mom about and since I really wasn't connected with my Dad, I did what everybody else did: I watched what the boys on the street did and of course, I got the "right" answers from my crew.

Cuda and Jake were my closest friends and for the next few years, our lives would be interwoven. There was no better feeling than to have them on the basketball court with me when we played three-on-three against other boys. On the courts, we all had our roles: I was the scorer; Jake was the one who grabbed the rebounds and passed the ball to me, while Cuda was our best defender. His job was to stop the other team's best scorer. We worked as a team.

Together we would figure out many things about life, especially what made girls tick and why we were all thumbs when it came to them. Just remembering the way we treated girls, I now see how they could develop a lack of trust in men. Wow, we really had no idea how what we considered as fun would affect the rest of a girl's life.

Around our neighborhood, you could recognize a true playa by his ability to get with as many girls as he could. Neither my boys nor I were even close to that playa status but for me this would change a little later. Back then, we worshipped the brothers who openly flaunted their playa status. If we were honest, we would admit that we wanted to be playas, and we'd do it at whatever cost.

Most of the guys in my neighborhood, like me, didn't have their dads around, so the playa was the man we commonly acknowledged as our role model. The ironic thing was that the playas themselves often had many children by several different women and were the same kind of dads to their children as our dads were to us! The very thing that we despised in our dads, we admired in the playas. It seemed the more babies the playas had, the more popular they became with the fellas.

Now, Cuda, Jake and I, we weren't any real threats to the playas in our 'hood'. We couldn't even "close the deal" with any of the neighborhood girls. We were inexperienced and scared all at the same time. So, we did what any group of 13-year boys would do: we got together and talked about all of the girls we wanted. We all secretly wondered and bragged out loud about who would be the first fool to venture into the foreign territory known as sex. In our minds, having sex was like winning ten million dollars. We believed it was possible, but none of us had ever done it.

The more we talked about it, the more alluring it seemed to us. Many things appear alluring initially but can have lasting effects well after satisfying that appetite. You know, the apple in the Garden of Eden had to have looked great and I'm sure it even tasted wonderful. Yet, a brief departure from doing what should be done had a resounding effect on every human being. All they wanted was a bite of an apple, and all we wanted was a girl our age that would let us experience all of the things we heard from the true playas. What could be the harm in that?

For Cuda, Jake and me, our thoughts only focused on the enjoyment because that's all the fellas talked about. The fellas never talked about there being any consequences for having sex. The unwritten, but followed, rule was that the baby was the female's problem to deal with and playas, we aspired to become, just continued to play. If someone got pregnant then the playa just moved on to new territory. You know, I always wondered why the mothers in my neighborhood were so strict on their young daughters but let the boys run wild. Hmmm? Still don't know why, but that sure is what was going on in my neighborhood and we tried desperately to get in on all of that play'n.

We lived in an environment where there were absolutely no repercussions for our actions as it related to male-female relationships. My father had proven that by walking out on us and going on with his life. "Like father like son." Everybody always said that I was a chip off the old block but I never could really see how I was like him. I could never be like him, or so I thought.

All of the guys from my childhood viewed girls like basketball. Both basketball and girls were ways to validate your status as a man and to enhance your rep. A girl's feelings meant nothing to the fellas. You were just supposed to play with a girl's feelings to get what you wanted and this boosted your rep, and if a girl got her feelings hurt, that was her problem. Largely, we were products of our environment. At that time, we weren't thinking about the weight of our actions on our lives, we were just looking for a piece.

I knew many young men who openly bragged about the number of children they had around town, but not many of them ever mentioned that they were actively involved in their children's lives. The fellas only focused on how many women they laid. There is a great difference between fathering a child and being the father of the child and I knew that better than most, but most fellas in my 'hood' wanted or needed the respect of the other fellas in the 'hood'.

The fastest and easiest way to earn that respect was by running the girls. Somewhere deep down I knew it was wrong but I hadn't developed the strength to go against the grain, so I tried to fit in and did just what the fellas expected me to do.

Besides, I remembered what it was like to be alone, an outcast, so to speak, and now I was finally building a group of friends and I really didn't want to nor could I afford to jeopardize them. I gave in to peer-pressure. This pressure was real.

There were times when I really liked a particular girl and would rather be with her than running with the fellas, but doing that would go against the code. I had to be hard, run with the fellas, and see the girl when our schedule would permit. There was a time Cuda was really digging this girl, Cindy, and he cut Jake and I off. Man, we rode him relentlessly. He didn't pay us any attention and did what his heart told him. Shoot, deep down, I respected him for that. I think I may have even been envious because he had a girl and Jake and I didn't. Cuda's relationship seemed to be going strong and it appeared that our threesome would soon become a twosome.

Over time, Cindy ended up dropping Cuda and we let him back into the fold without much of a fuss. You see when you are boys; you are there for each other during good times and bad. More than that, Cuda made our trio complete, so it was good to have him back on board with us. I thank God I came out of the stage of being insecure and not giving the right value to women; although this process would result from getting a taste of my own medicine.

PLAYA VS HUSTLER

Now, even though the playa in our neighborhood got mad respect on the street, there was one that got more recognition than he did: the hustler: The hustler clearly stood head and shoulders above everyone else. To be honest with you, the hustler had to combine the energy of the best athlete and the skills of the best playa in order to make money. The hustler needed quick thinking to make split-second decisions necessary to stay ahead of the competitors and the law.

He had to have the physical and mental agility to navigate through many neighborhoods and situations every day so that he could make a profit. The hustler had to be able to deal with all kinds of people, because contrary to popular belief, people from all walks of life are involved in the hustle game: they are either a consumer or a proprietor. The hustler required the ability to foster a sense of comfort and confidence with those he came into contact. These skills were essential for success.

From my neighborhood, there weren't too many folks going to college or who had management positions, so some used the hustle game to establish their credibility – their worth. A hustler was their own CEO and was at the top of their small business, and in some cases, it was big business. Some of these folks were savvy businessmen. They could have done well in any profession if they focused on the right things.

Although we had some legitimate hard-working folks, one side of my family had its share of hustlers as well. It was difficult for me to see them make daily choices that allowed them to make fast money in a short period while I watched Mom struggle just to make ends meet. Morally challenged, I had some choices to make because the lure of fast money and the things it provided was and continues to be a powerful temptation for anyone, especially a kid like me. Besides, people saw most of the hustlers as cool people; they did not come off as mean or cold. Most of them were very well liked, and just seen as someone trying to make a dollar. But I learned that being friendly is part of the hustle, part of the distortion needed to survive that lifestyle.

The hustlers in my neighborhood were fun loving and giving people. Always ready to toss some spare change to the younger kids. They would do things like sponsor a community barb-a-que or basketball tournament. I think it was their way of giving back to the rest of us. In some ways, doing these things could have provided the hustlers a sense of justification for their actions. If you do good things around your neighborhood then you really couldn't be that bad. Right? Regardless of their reasons, these guys were the ones who had the juice around town.

I knew that I didn't want to be caught up in the game the hustler had to endure, but I sure did like the benefits they got from being in the game…well, the benefits they flaunted before us. These guys had their choice of the girls and heck, I was a teenaged boy watching these fellas pulling the finest girls without any effort. It just made me scratch my head. On top of all of that, the hustler had the best rides and girls always lined up hoping to get a ride. Now, most of my friends and I took the city bus wherever we wanted to go, so there weren't many girls falling at our feet to roll with us.

I tried to get my hustle on, too…legitimately. I caddied at the local golf course and did other odd jobs trying to keep money in my pockets. But the girls had a choice; they could try to catch the eye of a sharply dressed, smooth talking, nice ride-driving hustler, or hang out with me on the bus. They didn't run to be associated with a sweaty caddie. That baffled me to no end. I was at least trying to do the right thing! There were a couple of hustlers who told me they wanted to help me out by letting me work for them and I started to think, "What's the harm in putting some quick money in my pocket?"

The funny thing about the hustler was he rarely had anything to show for his efforts. I mean most of them never moved out of the neighborhood or upgraded their standard of living. They spent the money as fast as they received it. The only visible evidence of increased income for the hustler was through the new cars, clothes, and jewelry they flaunted. Why did they drive these nice cars and still live in the projects? Why didn't they move out of the projects? For a fact, I knew that I was taking the first chance I have to get out of the neighborhood. So, maybe I was already one up on the hustler. Yet, there was still something inside of me that said, "Maybe it could help me get out quicker." What's a brotha to do?

CHAPTER TWELVE
SMELLING MYSELF

Besides Jake and Cuda, the only other folks I hung out with were upperclassmen. I wanted to do what they did, go where they went, and my grades suffered. They had all their credits and could afford to run around. I didn't have all of my credits and needed every one I could earn. Boy, did my grades suffer. So, my routine was to beat my mother to the mailbox and get my grades out before she could see them. Of course, she always checked with the school to find out what my grades were. At least I bought myself a little time, but then I'd be in trouble.

The more I hung with the upperclassmen, the less I was interested in school. I was hanging out with these guys when I started to skip school and get into different things. I had my first taste of Malt Duck while skipping school with these guys. I really didn't like how it tasted, but I figured I had to find out why they were all hyped about it. The thing was that I could have just asked my brother for some because he always kept a bottle hidden somewhere around the house. Heck, I didn't want him to know I was drinking; besides, eventually the novelty of drinking with them wore off and I would just hang with them.

Now, I remember missing a whole lot of classes but there were never any notices sent home, so I felt like I was in the clear, or so I thought. Then I realized final grades were coming out and I knew I was in serious jeopardy of staying back. There was no way I wanted to repeat the ninth grade again. No one was going to make fun of me the way we made fun of those kids who were kept back a year. The jokes and comments were harsh and I had no stomach for this kind of treatment, especially not when I would be the target.

This was like my worst nightmare coming true. I knew my mother would kill me.

I checked the mail every day for the final report card hoping that I made it. I had taken six classes and had to pass four of them to go to the tenth grade. Finally, the envelope showed up and I was too afraid to open it. Right then I pled with God. Begged Him, albeit too late, but begged that if I passed this time, I would do much better next year. Now, if I didn't pass, there wouldn't be much for me to worry about because my mother was going to kill me. I was sweating all the way through the process. But when I saw the report; my final grades were four Ds and two Fs.

I had never been so glad to get a D in my life. I ran to my back porch and proceeded to burn that report card. The remainder of my high school years, I was an honor roll student, and I never had to burn another report card. I left the hustlers and upperclassmen alone and focused on my promise to God to do better. Although my academics were now under control, there would be other interesting experiences to go through.

Like with most men, sex has been a major influence in my life. Hearing about it, dreaming about it, wanting it, getting it, the drive for sex can provide both pleasure and oftentimes pain at differing times. Early on, I realized it is the one appetite that must be controlled if I ever wanted to realize my full potential, but once unleashed, it was difficult for me to corral the sexual beast that lay just under the surface. My entree to this insatiable desire for sex occurred the summer of 1980, right after my freshman year. Until that time, my primary interests were athletics and normal boyhood endeavors, then came that fateful day when things would never be the same again.

Like many things before and after then, peer pressure played a big role in the decision to lose my virginity. My brother Joey knew I was dating this girl named Audrey and would constantly ask me about if I had "done it" with her yet. Of course, I hadn't done it or even felt comfortable about the prospect of having sex. Now to make things worse, let's just say that Audrey was not as naive about sex as I was. As a matter of fact, my cousin Darrin had done it with her before. So, this created even more pressure because this was seen as a sure-fire deal. After a while, I got tired of him riding me about why I couldn't close the deal.

One day my brother cornered me. He knew I was afraid do it with Audrey, he also said I was weak. He even went so far as to bet me some money that I couldn't do it. I knew I could not let him think he was right; furthermore, I was in no position to be paying out any money, so my task was clear. It's amazing how pride and the fear of ridicule can make people do things they never planned to do.

Kissing and hugging was the only thing I had ever done with Audrey and I did not intend to go any further, but the constant needling of my brother began to sink in deeply. Joey planted the seed and it began to take root in my mind of how I would actually pull off what was going to be one of the defining moments of my life. Getting her to my house was no problem; she always was available to come for a visit. This particular afternoon was different from the others, the house was empty, it was hot, and so were we. I went into my usual routine of kissing, touching, and feeling but I knew this day would be different. We were in my brother's room, which was in the back of the house; this gave us the best chance to get ourselves together if someone came in unexpectedly. I'm not sure if it was the heat or the excitement that caused me to sweat so, but I was drenched. I tried to act as if I was comfortable with what was going on but my heart was pounding so loudly, that I just knew she could hear it. An obvious knot in my throat surfaced from time to time and I tried to calm myself.

Audrey appeared to take pleasure in my awkward attempt to seduce her. I continued to fumble with her clothing; unable to do anything right, I clearly was out of my league. A smart person would have stopped; however, I was not a smart person that day. Excitement and curiosity had taken the place of discretion and common sense. Audrey seemed to sense I was ready to go for it and she started to undress right in front of me. The sight of her undressing caused the knot in my throat to surface again but now the size of a baseball.

There she stood naked with no inhibitions or fear, with an inviting look on her face. It soon became clear that she was beckoning me to do the same thing. I had never taken my clothes off in front of anyone like this and I was petrified. I fumbled around with my pants for what seemed like forever. I looked down at the buckle and zipper that were betraying me. How could something that I had done for hundreds of times have become such a very challenging act? As I continued to struggle, Audrey stood there with an amused smile on her face; what she saw entertained her. Eventually I got them off and I wanted to dive right under the covers but she would not let me. She guided me to sit with her on the bed, on top of the covers. I felt uncomfortable, excited, and nervous at the same time. She grabbed my hand as she lay down on the bed and I could feel sweat beading up on my forehead. She knew I was a virgin and took pleasure in watching me in my uneasy state.

I was totally out of my element and had no clue on what to do next, but on the other hand, she knew exactly what to do and guided me into an unknown place. All the excitement that led up to this moment was overwhelming. I had no idea of what I was doing and less thought about how she felt about what I was doing. All I can remember thinking about was the fact that I was now doing what the fellas and I always talked about doing. Man, I could officially start comparing myself to some of the playas in the neighborhood because now I had some credibility.

Before I could get any further in my thoughts, the thrill of the moment got the best of me. As quickly as it began, it was now over. Something was happening that I had never experienced and I wasn't sure what to do about it. A rush of adrenaline surged through my body and my only thought was to ride this wave of energy. These feelings caused my body to jerk and twist beyond control. I felt embarrassed because I'm sure Audrey must have thought I was having a seizure. "Dang, how much longer could this go on because I didn't know how much more I could take," I thought to myself. It soon began to subside, the newfound feelings left my body, and I was able to catch my breath again. We both lay in bed for a while after we were done. There were no words exchanged, as I tried to process what had just taken place. For that moment in time, I felt like I was the man! Then I thought, "There had to be more to this than what just happened."

After that, things seemed awkward between Audrey and I; our communication became strained. Audrey and I eventually went our separate ways soon after that. I think I was just another virgin to whom she introduced to a new world. Now, I've heard different people talk about how your first time was supposed to be special, a once in a lifetime situation to be seriously pondered. How when you have sex the first time you give away something you can never get back. I didn't understand it at the time but I had a feeling that something happened and I would never be the same. Audrey didn't mean anything to me and I soon realized that I didn't matter much to her either. My mother still thought I was a virgin and if she ever found out I wasn't she would be hurt. Maybe I should have listened to those who said to keep myself pure, but the voice of the streets won out this time. All of a sudden, I didn't feel like a playa anymore, I was just confused. The money I would have lost to my brother would have been much better than the price I paid in life all because I let the beast out of the corral.

CHAPTER THIRTEEN
DRIVING FORCE

Jake was not going to compromise his dreams. Soon he managed to pick up a Ford Granada, which became our ticket to the world outside our neighborhood. Of course, it cramped our riding style when Jake had a girlfriend, fortunately for us, it took Jake a while to overcome his fear of women, so we usually had a ride.

Cuda was also a diligent young man; his entire family had a work ethic I admired. From the time I first met Cuda, he was always working some type of job to keep money flowing. I was the one who at times showed reluctance for going out and bringing in the dough. They would hassle me from time to time because I was the one who seemed never to have a steady job. I think that maybe my experience working for my Uncle Aaron traumatized me, but heck, one excuse sounds as good as the next.

Jake and Cuda were also exploring new things when it came to girls and we would get together and compare notes. I had a mad crush on Jake's sister, Rene during our high school years. Jake nearly had a conniption! To say the least, he was totally against us hooking up. He knew all too well how we tried to sneak around with girls and he didn't want me doing that to his sister. This situation created a small amount of tension between us, because he refused to understand that I saw Rene differently than the other girls. No matter what I said or did, he would not buy it, so I just let it go. His friendship meant more to me than a passing fling. I must admit though, if I were him, I wouldn't have believed me either.

Jake knew all too well that I would do anything if I wanted a woman. I remember having a crush on this girl Crystal. I went through all kinds of changes just to be near her. She loved to act and was always in school productions. Man, I ended up trying out for a play just to be near her. It scared me to death when I actually got a decent part in one of the plays. Although my motives weren't the purest, I realized that I loved acting. Crystal never gave me the time of day but I was happy to be close to her during rehearsals.

In another attempt to get closer to the ladies, I tried out for the basketball team in my junior year in high school. Now, you have to keep in mind, I stood a flat five foot nothing and only had desire and heart on my side. Unbelievably, I made the team! Just as shocked as everybody else, I couldn't hide my excitement. No one believed I could make the team even I had my doubts. Being on the team was a huge nugget I carried around with pride. In our neighborhood, you were the man if you could play ball. The fine cheerleaders that lined up to perform in front of the team were just a bonus that kept my mind twirling as they flipped and jumped their way into my dreams. I could never break into their ranks, but it was fun trying.

Things were changing all around me and I was still just out to have fun. Jake always knew that he wanted to be a lawyer, so he was working hard to keep his grades up. Cuda was doing well in trade school and many of my other partners were either working or in college. My grades were good but I had no idea of what I wanted to do. This began to make me nervous because I did not want to be like many of the men in our neighborhood who were full of promise but for one reason or the other, they just hung out because they didn't have any plans for their lives. Reality started to set in and I knew that I would soon have to make decisions about the rest of my life. There was always the hustle game, and I must admit there were times when I considered trying to make the fast money.

There were a couple of the hustlers who had taken a liking to me and wanted to get me started. The lure of money and the things that came with it could solve my immediate problems of what to do after high school. I began to ponder if I could do it without my mother finding out; my thinking was that the money I took in could help around the house. Though deep down I realized if she found out, I would be a part of something that would hurt her and the thought of that was too much for me. She had done so much for Joey and I, and I could not let all of my mother's efforts go to waste. Besides, I saw where the hustlers eventually ended up and I wanted more than that for my life.

I knew deep down I was not ready for college; I lacked the desire and discipline to get there. I also knew my family did not have enough money to help me if I went to college, so I did not even talk about it. To make things worse, my father and I were becoming more and more agitated with one another. The world I'd so carefully crafted for myself was starting to close in around me.

CHAPTER FOURTEEN
WHAT ARE YOU GOING TO DO NOW?

We were nearing the end of our senior year in high school; Mt. Saint Mary's College in Maryland already accepted Jake and he would soon be leaving. A few months earlier during a career day at school, the armed forces recruiters had us take entrance exams to see if we could qualify for the military. I scored well enough to qualify for whatever branch I wanted to enter, but to be honest, I had no real desire to do military service, and I don't even know why I took the test. Cuda took the test as well and he had an acceptable score. The Air Force was the branch that really pursued me but I had never left home and wasn't planning on leaving. I worked a few odd jobs during this time in a couple of restaurants and soon realized I had no future in food services. All of that standing up and smiling to obnoxious customers was just too much for me to bear.

My manager at the International House of Pancakes would always say, "The customer is always right." To me, many of the customers were just trippin' and I wasn't paid enough to deal with their crap. Longevity on the job was never a strong suit for me and normally, I would come home after a couple of weeks. In some cases, it was only a matter of a few days before I'd be out of a job. It always seemed to tear off pieces of my heart when I had to tell my mother I either quit or was fired. Once when I worked at McDonalds, I remember going work to check the schedule for my next shift and not finding my name on the roster. The manager simply said, "I'll need the hat back when you come back for your last check." Man, that was cold. We were about to graduate and everyone had something in the works for the future but me. I avoided conversations about my plans and future because I didn't have a clue or a plan.

I had to do something soon because, after a couple of years of Dad being around, I felt bad about putting pressure on Mom to allow him back. Dad and Joey started to have issue after issue and I could tell that it wouldn't be long before things erupted into a violent end. More and more, it was a struggle to communicate and I think I was going through my teenage rebellious stage where I wanted to be a man – "smelling myself" as the older people used to say. For me, the final straw with Dad came when we were joking around one day and I said, "If you ever tried to hurt me, I would call the police." Before I knew what happened, Dad hit me in the face! BAM! "What the...." I thought.

I was going on 17 at this point, and I can look back vividly and remember the pain. I did not shed a tear, I just looked at him, and I think we both knew that was the last time he would ever put his hands on me. Joey was "hot" about that incident and we briefly had conversations on how to even the score and get away with it. It seemed like everything was closing in around me. I was getting close to graduating from high school and I had no plan. To compound the problem, I knew that staying in our house was not going to work because of the mounting tension between Dad and I.

If I couldn't get what I needed from Dad or at home, I knew I would get it from somewhere else. For an adventurous teenager, the somewhere else, when not from Uncle Aaron or Uncle Robert, was often from hanging out with the fellas on the street. However, the lessons learned in the street can be fast and dangerous. Lessons learned outside the home can often leave the pupil changed forever, and in many cases not for the better.

Graduation came and went. I was proud and terrified at the same time. When you turned eighteen in my family, they broke your dinner plate and you had to find a way to feed yourself. I knew I had to do something. I needed counsel so I ran to a place I have always loved; I went to the beach.

I felt peace in the solace of admiring nature and the beauty in it. At the beach, I listened to myself and found solitude with God in nature.

Sitting on the pier, I noticed how the waves of the ocean made it to the land's edge no matter what tried to impede its progress. The water hedged over, around or through whatever was in its way. For me, the ocean was a place where the world and its distractions were forced out and my natural senses were enhanced. Sitting at the ocean increased my ability to hear, there was no hustle and bustle of the city drowning out nature's serenade. It was just me and God and I needed to hear. God spoke and I was able to hear. I had my answer. It was time for me to get out of my comfort zone.

The ocean was right, I couldn't look at the obstacles in life as a negative, but I had to look at them as opportunities on which to build and prosper. I knew there was something out there for me and I had to try to chase after my dreams. Sitting at the mouth of the world, I decided to go into the Air Force.

Nobody, I mean nobody took my thoughts of leaving seriously. But the day the Air Force recruiter showed up to my house to get my parents signature, because I was 17 when I signed up, they knew then that I was not kidding. I signed up in August 1983 and would leave in January 1984. This was my last summer at home; soon I'd leave to discover a world of new things. I was only a man-child but would be the one to fly the coop – the one that really got away. Could anyone tell that I was proud and terrified all at the same time?

My last summer was tough because it was full of good-byes. We only had a few months before Jake left to go to college and I left for the Air Force. I had a few more odd jobs, which kept money in my pocket, before I left for basic training. One of which was working as a security guard at a local factory. My job was to periodically walk around this plant and make sure everything was under control. Yeah, I'm sure everyone around there felt safe when they saw my imposing, five-foot, four inch, 118 pounds of menacing presence thunder through the place.

To ensure I was making my rounds, they gave each guard a key to insert into time clocks located throughout the plant. This registered the time the guard made rounds. There were about 20 of these clocks and the rounds had to be done each hour, man that was a lot of walking. My shift supervisor was a career security guard who in my opinion was taking his job much too seriously. We called him "Sarge." He would always tell me how he was ready to react to any emergency, and fully capable of subduing any would-be offender. For me, this was just a way of keeping some spare money in my pockets until I left for the Air Force. I had to remind Sarge that my goals were not connected to the factory but connected to what the Air Force had for me. Each time I'd tell him this, he would say "Boy, if you stay here in about 20 years you could be like me." This really scared me.

When it came to making the security checks around the factory, he was always pulling rank on me. One day I asked him why he never made any rounds. He stated, "I got seniority and you don't have any, so make the rounds boy." I never remember him getting out of his chair unless he needed a bathroom break. I wondered if he even knew his way around the factory, because all he did was eat his smelly sandwiches and tell me how much of a trained killer he was. Sarge was from Barbados and said he prepared all his own food for work, and that his sandwiches were a family secret. Now, in my opinion, it was a secret that I hoped he'd never share with me, and I encouraged him to keep his sandwiches at home. I never did figure out what was in those sandwiches, I just knew when he pulled them out of the bag it was time for me to make my rounds.

As far as being alert and agile, Sarge was anything but. He had the Dunlap disease, that's where your stomach done lapped over your belt. We wore these brown security guard uniforms and he was a sight to see in his. The buttons on the shirt were stressed to the point where it looked as if they would explode away from the material. In between the buttons, you could see his undershirt beneath due to the stretching of the shirt. His pants were way too tight, showing bulges and imprints that no one wanted to or should have seen. Not only tight, but his pants were high waters, as well, exposing the white tube socks he wore daily. Sarge was always pulling at his crotch area trying to free the material from bunching up. I tried to remind him that the security company we worked for would issue us new uniforms. His response was "Ain't nothing wrong with my uniform, I'm in regulation." I could not believe he didn't realize how goofy he looked.

Now if he ever had come from behind his desk, I knew there were a couple of reasons Sarge could never catch a perpetrator. First, he wore these black security guard shoes with thick heels. There was no way he would be able to take more than a few steps without tripping. Secondly, Sarge had some of the thickest glasses I'd ever seen in my life. I had serious doubts Sarge could even identify a criminal, let alone stop one. When a person would come to our desk to gain entry to the factory, Sarge would have to get extremely close to them to read their badges. Some would recoil at the smell he had on his breath after eating one of his special sandwiches. I asked him how long had it been since he had his prescription checked for his glasses. He just yelled, "I got seniority in here and I ask the questions, now make your rounds boy."

He always bragged about his twenty-year career of catching criminals. But, when I asked him how many people had he apprehended, all he said was, "That's what's wrong with young people today, all they do is talk and not listen." My guess was that he was still trying to bag his first criminal. To add the final insult to my time out at the factory, one day I was doing my rounds and turning my keys when something happened. One of the clocks popped open and there was no tape inside to record the time. Ah heck! They didn't have any way of knowing if I was making the rounds or not! Shoot, from that point on I spent the rest of my time hanging on the loading dock cracking jokes with the fellas.

When it came time for me to quit Sarge, sat me down and told me how to survive in a wartime environment. I tried to figure out how he knew all of this since he had never been outside of Stamford. He said, "You need to watch the Viet Cong when you get over there." Now, he knew I was going to Texas for basic training but I learned not to correct Sarge, so I continued to listen to his war advice. I let him have his moment and tried to appear to be attentive because I knew he really liked me and I had begun to like Sarge as well. It really hit me that I would be leaving home soon. Secretly, I looked forward to hanging out with Sarge and his crazy ways and stories. We said our good-byes and from time to time, I reflected on him and missed his stories but not his sandwiches.

Jake was supportive of my decision to go to the Air Force and Cuda said he was going to go with me. We had another friend we called Boo who said he was going with Cuda and I. The limited opportunities in our neighborhood frightened me and the mounting tensions with Dad pushed me. I didn't want to live a mediocre life because of fear of the unknown. Fear had snuffed out many dreams; I didn't want it to rule out my dreams, too. The Air Force was my dream and I learned a valuable lesson at this time. I learned that in life, you sometimes have to be prepared to chase your dreams alone if necessary. You see, in the end, Boo ended up getting a girl pregnant, so he stayed home and worked at a gas station and Cuda backed out as well.

CHAPTER FIFTEEN
BRIDGES TO THE FUTURE - NEW FIRSTS

My time to leave home was at hand and I was starting mentally to prepare for an uncertain future away from home in the Air Force. My brother would stand in my face and scream at me like a drill instructor, he said this would get me ready for the real thing when the time came. I usually ended up laughing and I figured that if this indicated what basic training would be like then it too would be a joke. My uncle Morris was about to enter the Navy around the same time so we would jog together to get ourselves in shape for our new lives. I had a lot of hair back then and would get it cut shorter and shorter every week before I left home. My thoughts were that if it all had to come off at one time, the shock would have killed me. All of the physical preparations were easy compared to the emotional stress of leaving. I had no idea of what was about to happen in this next phase of my life. I was a mama's boy and had rarely been away from home for an extended time. So, this was definitely uncharted territory.

Saying goodbye to Cuda and Jake was tough. It was then I realized how much I loved them and relied upon their friendship. My brother tried to put on a strong image as I was leaving but I could see he was just doing what a man was supposed to do. I knew he would miss me and I would miss him as well. My brother and I never talked about how we felt about each other but we showed it. I never questioned his love for me. I began to reflect on the things he did for me like being there when I was terrified of death, going to the ropes, wanting to get even with my father for him hitting me, and even yelling at me like a drill instructor. These were his ways of trying to take care of me as his little brother. Then something puzzling happened that took years to understand it completely.

Leading up to my departure, my father became very quiet and withdrawn from me; I didn't make too much of it figuring he must have had something on his mind. The day I left, he refused to get out of bed. I sat down next to him on the bed and he would not come from under the covers. I could hear him crying. I looked at my mother, but all she said was that we needed to hurry up. I had never seen him cry before and didn't know how to react. I told him to take care and that I would call when I could.

I had all my favorite clothes and the prayers of my family and friends with me as I headed for the train station. My mother and brother took me down there; my father, still in bed when I left, was not able to muster the energy to get up. This was the first time I had witnessed a vulnerable side of my father. He really did possess a heart and had the capacity to feel. I wished I had seen it earlier; maybe things would have been different.

The ride to the station was mostly quiet. I guess we were all trying to figure out how this was going to play out. In my family, no one really left home and I found myself saying maybe I shouldn't either but it was too late for that now. I received my last words of encouragement and was just ready to get on the train. This saying goodbye stuff is painful and I was about to break down. I can still see my mother looking at me and hoping that I was ready for the world. I just wanted to make her proud and I figured if I looked back anymore that I'd be a mass of tears. So, I did my best to present a confident image, waved farewell and strolled to the train, found my seat and proceeded to cry like a baby.

Life is full of ironies such as when I finally came home from the hospital after my bout with tuberculosis, I never wanted anyone to leave me, yet now I'm the one leaving. On top of that, I took my first flight as I headed to Texas to join the Air Force. I was hoping I would not freak out, but aside from my ears clogging, the trip went fine. Upon landing in San Antonio,

Texas, all the recruits were rounded up and put on a bus took bound for Lackland Air Force Base where for the next 6 weeks we would experience culture shock.

In the middle of the night, our bus finally came to a stop in front of the rows of barracks that dotted Lackland. A spit and polished Training Instructor (TI) boarded the bus and proceeded to tell us that he was our mamas and daddies for the next 6 weeks and we had better get used to it. Once off the bus we did this "pick 'em up and put 'em" down drill with our luggage for about five minutes. I wondered why this guy couldn't make up his mind.

There were about forty of us on the bus and they lined us up in four groups. The TIs began to ask us questions like where we were from and would always find some witty way to embarrass us after we responded. One guy said he was from Georgia and the TI said the only thing that came from there were steers and queers and wanted to know which one was he. My recruiter told me to try to blend in while I was at basic training and I quickly figured out why; those who stood out would be rode hard for their entire time.

Finally, they allowed us to settle into our bunks and get a good night's sleep, or so I thought. About 4:30 AM, we were awakened by the sound of an aluminum garbage can bouncing down the isle of or barracks. The TIs came in yelling and screaming to get moving and get downstairs for formation. We stayed on the third floor and we had to be up and in uniform, standing in formation in three minutes. This just seemed impossible; there is no way to be able to have your uniform looking good and boots on and in formation in that amount of time. So much for being able to blend in, I was always among the last to fall out. I was creating a problem for my peers because whatever element I lined up in could not eat until everyone was present and accounted. They only gave us five minutes to eat and if we were late lining up then, we had even less time. Some days by the time you received your food, the TIs were saying time to move out. I then tried to sleep in my uniform to be able to be ready for the 0430 formation, but this was not the best idea because another guy got caught doing this and was disciplined. I had to rethink that trick.

Our days were packed full of training, after breakfast we would have various appointments for things like getting our uniforms, taking shots, military studies classes, and drill to name a few. We would be busy until about 2030 and then we'd have 30 minutes for personal time before the 2100 lights out. I was miserable and seriously wondered if I had made a tremendous mistake. We were constantly taking test or having different forms of inspections. I was trying hard to stay up to speed with all the requirements but it became a constant struggle. I had failed one open locker inspection and the policy was that if you failed two inspections of any type you would be recycled through basic training again. I had been there for three weeks and I could not take starting over again. We had to take academic evaluations to graduate as well and I was having trouble staying awake in class.

One day I remember the TI screaming for the idiot who was sleeping to get up and stand in the corner and I started to move. Fortunately, he was referring to someone else and he did not see me, I made a vow to do whatever it took to stay awake. I gutted it out by biting my lip or pinching myself and never fell asleep again. Then, the unthinkable happened. We were in class and the instructor said we would be having a no-notice open locker inspection right after class. I knew that my clothes were not ready and that meant I would be removed from my flight and recycled. I told my TI that I was not feeling well and asked to be excused for a moment and he bought it. I ran up to the barracks and put on three T-shirts and four pairs of underwear, these were the ones I did not have time to fold. So, I managed to pass the inspection and learned a trick or two. I went and purchased some extra underwear and had one of the other guys fold them for me and I never wore them, I just left them in my locker for inspection. I hid the others in the ceiling tiles and before I knew it, my time to leave this place was coming before my eyes. I was even among the first downstairs in the morning for formation.

Everyone has their own way of dealing with adversity and some did not handle this stressful place very well. Some guys would be calling cadence in their sleep, and all of us were homesick but we were starting to jell as a unit. As bad as I felt about being there, I did not want to come home a failure, although many of the fellas expected to see me any day. Graduation day came and we marched across the parade field with pride and I felt a sincere sense of accomplishment. I met some really nice guys and together we made it through. I found out my job in the Air Force would be a 702, which was an Administrative Specialist, a paper pusher. My celebration would be short lived because I had to go to Keesler AFB, MS for technical school to learn my new job.

Tech school was much more liberal than basic; it was more of an academic environment than basic training. I was doing well academically but I was having some serious problems typing, you had to be able to type twenty words a minute to be able to graduate. I knew this would be the make or break point for me because typing was not coming easy for me. I met some good folks as well while I was at school there and we would try to hang out when we were not studying.

One guy in particular, Argyle, (he always wore argyle and the nickname stuck with him) he was training for the same job as I was and we really clicked. Our lives would be intertwined for quite some time. Argyle was the lady's choice whenever we went out because he could sing like Jeffrey Osborne, and was a tremendous athlete with an engaging charisma. Immediately, I liked him; but he was the one who got me drinking beer on a regular basis. I never remember him studying but he always scored well on his tests. I had to buckle down because I had to get my typing up or I wasn't going to make it.

I tried to keep a positive light on my chances on passing my typing test and thought maybe getting off base would be a good diversion. Our instructors told us not to leave the base through certain gates because some of the locals did not like us. In 1984, people in the south still didn't have a problem letting you know that they didn't appreciate your presence. So, we went the way they said and I ended up at the mall with some friends. I could feel that I was not welcome and when I did buy something, the clerk made a point not to touch my hand. Placing my money on the counter and turning away as if I was some sort of inconvenience, I primarily stayed on base after that.

With my four weeks of tech school ending, I had to take my dreaded typing test. I had never even come close to doing well and I figured this would be no different. Lo' and behold, when I got my results, I had typed thirty words with only one error. Not only had I passed but also my overall class academic average made me the only honor graduate in my class.

I was floored, now the only thing left was to find out where I was headed to next. They would post everyone's duty assignment on the bulletin board in the hallway and when I looked, I was stunned, Mrs. B's little boy was going to Clark Air Base, Republic of the Philippines. I remember going to a map to see where it was located because I never heard of the Philippines before seeing it listed behind my name. Before leaving for the Philippines,

I went home for about two weeks to relax and catch up on what I had missed for the past three months. I had not realized it, but my experience away had broadened my perspective on life and introduced me to the many options available to me. I had developed a sense of pride for my accomplishments so far in the Air Force.

I PUT AWAY CHILDISH THINGS?

PHASE III

CHAPTER SIXTEEN
ON THE HORIZON

I remember wearing my uniform around the neighborhood; of course, I had to wear my shell toe Adidas with the fat shoelaces. Everyone seemed to be supportive and thought my uniform was cool, too. The Adidas made the uniform look tight. Now after seeing me, some of the fellas on the block said they were thinking about joining, of course none of them did.

My family expressed sincere happiness for me, for my future. My brief time away from home taught me that anything is possible if one can see outside their situation. Many of the people I grew up with never left home and based their life expectations on their knowledge of our town. I had formed in my own mind a sense of where I was going to end up and did not like the prospects. But, somewhere deep down I knew there had to be more out there somewhere and I was afraid of not finding out.

Of course, now everyone was giving me a pep talk on what to expect in a foreign country. Jake and Cuda came by a few times and we reminisced as well as thought about our futures. We were all men now, each with their own path to take and world to conquer. Being back with my boys again was great and I envied them having each other while I was headed to a place where I knew no one. We went to some of the local spots to hang out at night and it felt strange to leave the house and not have a curfew. I had a newfound freedom and didn't really know what to do with it. I had a girlfriend at the time named Jenny and she said she'd wait for me while I was gone. I thought that was cool, a guy always wants to have someone back at home when the times get rough.

I started to get anxious and nervous concerning what lay ahead of me in a foreign land and went to my place of refuge whenever I had problems —

the beach. The ocean represented serenity and peace, a place where I could always put things in the right perspective. The tide taught me about life; how it would always find a way to get around any obstacle placed in its way. I would look toward the horizon and see the place where it looked like heaven and earth became one and knew within myself that I could have a part of both inside of me. I was ready to go and face whatever life had in store for me; I had again found my balance in life.

A WHOLE NEW WORLD

Perception has a way of clouding the view of those charged to take action, but life has a way of clarifying things for us. While on leave, my brother and I ran into my cousin Chucky whom I hadn't seen in a while. When we were growing up, I really looked up to Chucky because he had some serious status around town. He seemed to have it all going for him and I was hyped just to be around him again.

As we approached him and before I could get into reminiscing about old times, he tried to sell me a tape player. He didn't ever recognize me! Dang! Not him, too.

Drugs and not just the pot they used when I was younger and trying to fit in with the crowd, hardcore drugs like cocaine and crack were tearing our city apart. It was hard for me see Chucky like this...he was really messed up. Drugs have a way of creating a metamorphosis in a person. He used to be vibrant and focused, but now, he was weak and wandering. Chucky stood before me as a living reminder of the depths of the hustle game. The game can pull you in quickly and bring you down even faster. Chucky didn't stay on top of his game, and the game got the best of him. He had become more bone than flesh and this was extremely sad to see. All I could do was try to reflect on the way I remembered him because seeing him the way he was gave me pain that I did not want to deal with.

The brief time I had left at home had taught me volumes on life beyond where I had grown up. I know if others are afforded the vision to see beyond their circumstances and surroundings the individual life choices being made could be drastically altered for the better. The media and largely we contribute to the perpetuation of the images and lifestyles being equated to urban America.

I again went through the ritual of saying goodbye but this time was not as bad as the first, I actually was sort of excited and ready to explore a new horizon. My mother gave me a case of condoms, 72 in the pack; I was wondering if she knew something that I didn't. There was no indication from my experiences that I would even need seven, let alone 72, but I didn't say anything. As far as I knew, she did not know I wasn't still a virgin. "She couldn't have known about Audrey, could she?" I was actually embarrassed; I mean how many guys have their mother furnish them with condoms.

Once again, it was time to get on a plane, this time I was in for a long journey ahead to the Philippines or the "P.I.," as it is referred to by those of us in the military. Fortunately, with all the traveling to Texas and back home, airplane travel seemed to get easier. However, this would be 12 hours in the air, so I definitely did a great deal of praying. Eventually, the plane landed at Clark Air Base and it must have been 90 degrees outside. It was April and I thought that if this was the spring, then I could wait to see what the summer will be like.

The first person I met was my first supervisor, Will Arnold; he took care of me off the bat. Soon after arrival, I got a room in the barracks on the other side of the base that was a considerable distance from where I worked. They did not have any openings in the dorms where I was supposed to stay, so I stayed with the aircraft maintenance folks. The walk to work was long and I was hoping I'd be able to move soon. Will got me settled in and then basically I was on my own. I had never been so home sick in my life. I listened to some of the cassette tapes I made before I left and they made me more miserable.

I was so lonely from being away from my family and friends that it caused me to second-guess my decision to join the Air Force. Stationed on this island in the Pacific seemed like the furthest and loneliest place on the planet. It felt as if time stood still, suspended in a desperate place of isolation. I cried myself to sleep on more than a couple of nights.

I had not met too many people yet and I didn't feel comfortable with walking up to strangers and striking up a conversation. Yet, I longed for any type of connection, hoping to break the depression that had become my constant companion, I wrote letters to everyone I could think of during this time. I wrote Jenny, at least, a letter a week. I'm sure they were pretty depressing, but eventually I ran out of letters to write and had to go out to see what the base was like.

I tired of my pity party, and forced myself to venture beyond my work and dorm environment. I figured most of the fellas would be in the gym and since I still loved basketball, I'd go and see what the local talent was like. Changing my routine and attempting to reach out was scary but I tried the alternative and knew I didn't want to continue to live in that private imprisonment. I needed to be paroled. When I walked into the gym one of the first faces I saw were familiar to me. The Air Force had also sent Argyle to the P.I. and I immediately felt better. He had arrived a few weeks before I did and was already making a name for himself. His ballin' skills had given him big respect among the fellas and the ladies followed his every move on and off the court. Around the same time, a new dorm opened up on the other side of the base and I was finally able to move and be closer to my job and most of the other folks my age. An added bonus was Argyle and I would now live in the same building. We began to venture out and discover many of the things our local community had to offer.

My roommate was Landon Bowe, he was about 5 years older than I was and he took me under his wing. He stressed to me the importance of staying on top of my job qualification training and tried to keep me out of trouble. The latter was a full-time job because Argyle and I were running at full speed into whatever was out there. After about a month, I was drinking alcohol almost every day and practically living in bars. In the P.I., if you could walk up to the bar, they'd serve you, no matter your age or how drunk you were. Before I knew it, I was sucked into a routine, which was unlike anything I had ever experienced or dreamed of in my life.

CHAPTER SEVENTEEN
FANTASY ISLAND

This place was like Fantasy Island; anything you wanted; you could have for a price. The area surrounding the base was impoverished and the main source of income was the fulfillment of the selfish pleasures of men. Everything was geared towards sex; shoot, even in the Airman's Club on base they had strippers perform at lunchtime. Guys would go downtown during the day and get what we called short times. This was when a woman would do whatever you wanted for about five US dollars. I never imagined what a few dollars could get you before I got here. I was living out what I thought to be a carefree, fun-filled life of enjoyment.

In 1984 rap was just coming on the scene, I would go to clubs, bust a few rhymes, and do my break-dancing routine, and the women loved it. Before coming into the Air Force, Jake, Cuda, and I practiced rhyming and I was good at it, too. When I wasn't rapping, the women would swoon from Argyle's singing and we'd be in the mix again. Through Argyle, I met PJ, he was also from Connecticut and he made a point of letting me know that when we met, but at first, I was cold to him. I think the main reason was that he was a threat to my established domain of women. I saw him before and it seemed like we were always bumping into each other while chasing women. One thing about men is that no matter how many women they may have, they do not like to share (or think that they are sharing) and I was no different. Deep down I believe I liked PJ the first time we met, but I had to claim my stake. Eventually we established a working relationship when it came to women. We figured between the three of us that we could run things at Clark.

We developed a reputation for being notoriously persistent when it came to chasing the women. We made a point of hanging out almost every night of the week. Sometimes it was difficult to keep up the pace, not to mention the demands it took on the body, but neither of us would ever admit it.

We were a democratic group and the majority ruled; this even applied to going out to party. The thing about us was that if one of us just wanted to chill for the evening the others would not have it, the other two would pressure you so much until you had no other choice but to go out to drink and party all night.

In the midst of all of this, I somehow managed to progress through the training upgrade on my job. To this day, I can't see how my personal indulgences at that time didn't impact my career. Our lives were based on excess and feeding our lust. We all were good workers and managed not to allow our crazy lifestyles affect us on the job, but when the workday was done, we were off to see what new conquest was waiting for us. Clearly, my off-duty activities were the focus of my life and after about four months, I was out of the condoms my mother had given me.

I was no longer thinking about home or those I had left; I stopped calling and writing because I was in the groove in the P.I.! Heck, at one point, so much time had gone by since I talked to my mother that she contacted the American Red Cross and had them locate me to contact her. My boss chewed me out and said I had better call my mother. Since that incident, I've tried to do a better job of keeping in touch with my mother.

As young men in a place that catered to us, we did all we could to exploit our new found freedom. Most of my friends had never been away from home and we were clearly running wild and not even considering any possible consequences. I felt like I was bulletproof and able to get out of any situation. I developed a few alias names because I was dealing with so many females and I didn't want my lifestyle to get back to my job.

We even viewed venereal disease (VD) as more of a joke and a mere inconvenience, which caused us to have to stop drinking for a few days. I remember going out to a club and running into one of my boys and being able to spot the telltale sign that they were burning, the term we used for having VD. Anyone ordering juice or soda was on fire and we went out of our way to make jokes out of it. They'd always say that in a couple of days, they'd be right back out there and the truth of the matter is that many times the person had been with so many women that he couldn't tell which one burned him.

We had no regard for others or ourselves for that matter, caring only about from where or whom our next laugh was coming. Many times, guys who were temporarily out of commission because of some types of VD would stop taking the pills when their symptoms went away. The doctors warned that this was dangerous because a lack of symptoms did not necessarily mean you were completely free of the disease. We learned that it was much easier for a man to detect when something is wrong, but for a woman, the doctors said that they could go for long periods before they are aware that anything is wrong with them.

Ladies stationed on the P.I. were victims, too. If a woman got Pelvic Inflammatory Disease (PID), they were oftentimes not aware that they were burnt; even a good friend of mine had to be rushed to the hospital due to PID. She was in bad shape and it took a while for her to get back on her feet again. We were all just running buck wild. Our mothers would have hung their heads in the shame of it all.

The We Funk Crew reigned in the Philippines

CHAPTER EIGHTEEN
RUNNING WILD

Things picked up for me and after being there for about a year, I was completely out of control. I only focused on women, alcohol, and the nightlife while striving to keep things in line at work. Until this time, I manage to be proficient in all of my tasks, but the 24-hour party machine that took residence in my body was taking a toll on my performance at work. I think I was acting out just because there was no one looking over my shoulder. Deep down I would have struggled about some of the things I was doing but more times than not I would find a reason to keep running wild. Argyle, PJ, and I had the reputation for being the life of the party wherever we partied. Everybody wanted to hang with us and our crew became larger in a short period. We hooked up with a few more fellas and even formed our own variety show. We had singer, dancers, and rappers. Rap was the big thing back then, so you know I was one of the premier rappers in our crew. DJ's would spin the records and we would just cut loose.

Known, as the We Funk Crew, we traveled to different clubs on the island. It wasn't long before we became the toast of the town and even had a big show down in the capital, Manila. The notoriety we gained only increased our access to the things we wanted most — women and this modest taste of relative fame gave me the sense that we were immune to the things that existed around us. For a brief period, I thought that I was bulletproof from the ills of my environment, so I began to try to feed my growing appetite for self-indulgence.

All crewmembers were dogs. We even had a hierarchy and our own labels for the dogs within the crew.

We called the new kids on the block Buckaroos. They were just getting their feet wet to the life of women. Buckaroos were easy to spot because they had little or no discretion. They hooked up with anybody who would roll around with them. They bounced from woman to woman in hopes of closing the deal with somebody, anybody. The Buckaroo's lack of focus and direction often led to many lonely nights and as many cold showers. They represented the most basic elements of the unrefined and undisciplined breed of canine.

The next rung up the ladder was the Junior Veteran. This member had learned how to curb his enthusiasm and he didn't present an image of pure desperation when it came to a potential conquest. Mind you, there was no difference in appetite between a Buckaroo and a Junior Veteran, the difference was in how they carried out their quest. Now, when it came to juggling women in his life, the Junior Veteran still did not possess the ability to exercise seasoned patience. He didn't know how to hang in the club, scope out new options and still manage to keep his main girl happy.

Occasionally, the Junior Veteran would be involved in situations where more than one of his female companions would show up at the club – at the same time. This was never good. Sometimes things flared up in intense arguments that would end in a dousing of whatever the women were drinking. Of course, when this happened, the Buckaroo was always around in the role of the scavenger, there to feast on the fallout.

The Buckaroo and Junior Veteran were both considered dogs because dogs will run up on anything they can in order to please themselves. They rarely considered consequences or repercussions of their actions. If it smelled like it was available, they would do anything to run down the woman in question. The last group of fellas we hung out with in our crew was the Veterans.

Veterans controlled their passions and were able to manage their women. Many of these guys were married or in serious relationships. Veterans felt that men were put on this earth to conquer everything and everybody. From time to time they, too, would go on the prowl. But Veterans operated by strict rules and codes of conduct. First and foremost, Veterans always stressed taking care of home. They would never mess around with anyone who would jeopardize their serious relationship at home. I wondered how that was possible. They managed to have these outside relationships by being on top of the bills and making sure that the wife had whatever she desired. They always let the other women know about their main woman. That way they said the other woman would not have a reason to get upset because she knew the deal.

Veterans placed a greater emphasis on the physical elements versus the mental and emotional. They rarely went out and made sure that when they did that it counted for something big, such as a rendezvous with one of their women on the side. The Veteran usually did not have more than one woman on the side; no need in getting greedy. Although they were not above the occasional piece of strange, any woman that was new to you. She was a source of excitement, however, getting some strange was frowned upon because it was seen as an unacceptable risk and the Veteran was not one to take many risks.

During my Junior Veteran status, PJ, Argyle, and I hung out with a couple of Veterans. They said they saw potential in us and wanted to help us mature to the next level, so if they saw us being overzealous in our pursuits, they quickly corrected us. It always seemed like their correction came over a few beers that we had to buy. It was one of our duties to make sure the Veterans always had a cold one handy. The Veterans we hung out with were very resourceful. Not only did they have a way of getting us to pay for their drinks, they also used their creativity to quench their thirst for women.

Once the Veterans told me to develop a flyer stating that there was going to be a fishing trip sponsored by the base, they took these flyers and each of them placed one somewhere in their homes where they knew their wives would find them. Inevitably, the conversation would go something like this:

The wife: "Are you planning to go on this trip?" The Veteran: "Hmm, don't know, I'm thinking about it.... What do you think?"

Now, this was only a gratuitous offer, because they knew their wives weren't about to be in the sweltering sun, sitting in a boat all day, swatting mosquitoes. So, all of the wives relented and said that the Veterans should go, but they'd stay at home.

The plot continued: our jobs, as Junior Veterans was to procure a bus along with some nice ladies to accompany us on our trip to a secluded island just off the coast of the main island of the PI. We got a bus with a video recorder; a nice stereo system and the local girls provided some good food for the ride to our island getaway. The code name for the trip was **Toes in the Sand** or **TITS** for short. The rendezvous was taking shape and the Veterans were greatly appreciative for the arrangements. There were two major rules: 1) we could not ever discuss this trip once it was over, and 2) we **could not** bring any cameras. No cameras – no evidence. This alone told you that the Veterans were slick with their game.

I learned a lot from that day. They showed us how to be calculating and creative in getting over on the women in our lives. But, in the end, I realized a couple of things:

Veterans, as much as I hated to admit it, were dogs, too. They were just well-groomed dogs, but fully capable of the same behavior displayed by the Buckaroo and Junior Veteran. They considered themselves smooth and refined but like the old saying goes you can put icing on dog do-do but that won't make it a cupcake. In the end it is what it is, no matter how much you dress it up, these brothers thought they had graduated to a higher level, but in fact, they had regressed. If they were so smooth, then why were they hanging out with a bunch of young guys like us?

Deep down I knew I really didn't want to be a Veteran because what's the use of settling down if you're not going to settle down. Internally, I hoped eventually to outgrow these childish ways. The Veterans represented the elements of a brother who hadn't grown up yet. No matter how many women I had or where I hung out, I knew I didn't want to be out in this lifestyle for the rest of my life. I needed to grow up.

Slowly around me, I started to see the effects of the choices that were being made by some of my friends. A few of them were popped for doing drugs, they were kicked out, and I never saw them again. Drugs were just as prevalent as women were and, in many cases, the fellas couldn't walk away from the easy access. A momentary lapse in judgment can be so devastating.

It saddened me to see people I knew and liked booted, sent back to the states because of a lapse in judgment. It seemed like such a waste. The difficulty in this experience lied in the fact that I formed some close bonds with some who were popped. Sure, before they left, we'd say we were going to keep in touch, but deep down I knew that it was over. Other judgment issues saw a couple of them get women pregnant. Shoot, this was one of my greatest fears. I could hardly take care of myself, so how could anyone expect me, or anyone of us, to take care of a baby and the baby's mama. Wow, yeah at first, all of our fun just seemed harmless, but thinking about these other possibilities; things were starting to look a little different.

CHAPTER NINTEEN

WINE, WOMEN & SONG

Women, alcohol, and male hormones were a combination creating a tremendous amount of havoc in the lives of us during this period. Argyle, PJ, and I had our share and probably other's share of women during our stay together in the P.I. I remember meeting some really, high-quality people who I think could have been good in my life. However, when you are focused on yourself and filling your appetite, you may miss the better things in life.

Even between PJ, Argyle, and myself the unthinkable had happened; Argyle had fallen in love with one of the local girls outside the gate. We thought there was an unwritten rule that no female would ever come between us. Not only had she come between us but Argyle had even moved in with her and any attempt to talk to him about this just turned into an argument. PJ and I wanted the third part of our trio back in place so we had to come up with a plan.

PJ believed that Argyle's girl had a wandering eye and he set his sights on exploiting it. Over a period, we would visit them at their house and Argyle's girl, Marisol, became very comfortable with the two of us. She would prepare dinner for all of us and we'd hang out with them until it was time to go home to prepare for work. Argyle was purchasing major appliances such as washer and dryer, microwave oven and other home furnishings. This was way too much for our 19-year-old minds to process. Even if he didn't know, PJ and I knew that there was no way that Argyle should be tied down like this. His focus should have been on running with us and living the life of a young man and there was no room for a girlfriend.

Opportunity for us to impact their love nest soon presented itself. Argyle had to go out of town on a work-related trip and PJ and I formulated the particulars of our plan. PJ stopped by the house to check and see if Marisol needed anything. Lesson #1, never allow another man to check on your girl when you are out of town. PJ slowly gained the confidence of Argyle's girl and she began to confide in him regarding matters of the heart. Lesson #2, only discuss something between the two people involved in the relationship. All of this helps to keep boundaries clearly defined for those outside the relationship.

Eventually, the time was right and PJ made his move. Marisol did not put up much of a defense and PJ ended up sleeping with her. It wasn't even about sex with Marisol, PJ figured out what her emotional needs were and met them. Now, the other portion was to discuss this with Argyle when he returned from his trip.

Eventually Argyle got back and we both sat him down and told him what happened so that he would dump Marisol. He looked at us with a puzzled expression and said, "How could you both do something like this to me?" He didn't want to discuss it with us anymore, only wanting to see her to discuss what happened. I guess he really loved her and he wanted to go back and work past her infidelity.

We told him that we believed she was no better than the many other women that we routinely passed around and that he needed a wake-up call. He was devastated by our assessment of Marisol and I believe disappointed in the two of us for letting him down. We believed that we were helping him. I guess if someone is going to sneak around with your woman it should be someone other than a friend; but in our warped sense of right and wrong, we thought we were saving him from a deeper hurt later. The fear of losing his friendship over this was real in my heart and I hoped we could get past this. Argyle looked at PJ and me, said, "I don't even want to look at you two right now," and stormed off. We just stood there with nothing to say as he went to reclaim his relationship.

As I look back, I don't see Marisol as a bad person, just one who was mixed up and made a few bad choices just as we did. We sat there judging her for being weak and plotted to take advantage of this situation, but never looked at our own petty weakness and jealousy. I guess we didn't do any good at all in this situation. Eventually, Argyle got over his hurt, however things between him and Marisol cooled off significantly. Every time he saw her, thoughts of her being with PJ haunted him. Once again, the three of us resumed our routine and our relationship was becoming less awkward. With no threat of any women coming between us, things seemed calm again, but then there was a bigger scare to come along. As I mentioned earlier VD was almost an acceptable risk of doing business in the P.I. However, we started to hear about this new disease, AIDS, and it was straight-up killing people. Anybody stationed in the P.I. that was diagnosed with this one would be rushed off the island and taken to a treatment facility before they discharged them from the Air Force.

They made all of us attend briefings to hear about AIDS and it scared me to death because it took a while before you could be sure if you had contracted it or not. We were required to take a test to determine if we were positive or not. The flood of people and situations I had encountered rushed into my mind and painted a scary picture. Fear became a constant annoyance; if this result were positive, then life would be a living nightmare. The results took a few weeks to come in and immediately after the test was taken, I had a great deal of trouble sleeping and resting. Never experiencing a cold sweat before the day, the test was administered.

Just like the term says, you actually sweat but it is cold and causes you to shiver. I prayed to God like I had never prayed before then. When the fellas would get together, there was a sense of doubt with each of us. No one had the courage to bring up this terrifying topic. We didn't want the others to know we were concerned or considered a candidate for this deadly disease. So, we all were left to suffer in our anguish alone and exclusively. I had never been more afraid in my life. All of a sudden, those one-night stands didn't seem so cool anymore.

CHAPTER TWENTY
DUSTY: REAL LIFE LESSONS

Around this time, I met a man who would influence me in a deep and lasting way. He was simply known as Dusty. He came to the island around the same time that I did and for some reason, he took an interest in me. Dusty didn't hang out with the same crew as I did, but when I'd run into him from time to time, he would always have some encouraging words for me. Dusty was 21 years older than I was but had the ability to relate to what I was going through. He had been to the P.I. many years ago and had traveled the roads that I was on and knew what lay ahead for me and he was just trying to guide me through and around some of the traps that I was bound to face. We all need someone to guide and mentor us at our different stages in life, although I was afraid to reach out, Dusty wasn't afraid to grab me when I needed it.

Dusty was a tall, dark-skinned man with an imposing presence. His broad shoulders supported the thick neck he developed from years of lifting weights. Whenever he moved his powerful arms, they would flex instinctively. Touches of gray on his temples created a distinguished look of wisdom and my time with him would confirm that assumption. His light brown eyes were like reflecting pools and his piercing stare made it seem as if he were able to look through you. I hoped he could not see the real me because I knew he would be disappointed.

I knew deep down that hanging out with Dusty would be good for me but the draw of my newfound freedom and the pulse of the city's streets would force me to find excuses not to spend time with him. When I did hang with him, he always dropped nuggets of knowledge on me. Part of me wanted him just to give up on me; then I would not have to make excuses of why I didn't check in with him. Another part of me wanted him to keep pressing me. I guess I needed to know that he was going to be there for me in the end if, when I needed him. The funny part is that from the moment we met, I knew I needed him in my life.

My partners did not require much from me, just to kick it around and cover their backs when necessary. The thing about it was that Argyle and PJ were there whenever I needed them but let's face it, how much guidance can a person could expect from a 20-year old. For now, they were my partners, my road dawgs but they weren't like Cuda and Jake. Cuda and Jake were more like my brothers. What Argyle, PJ, and I had wasn't that deep. While on the P. I., I guess I felt more comfortable with these kinds of superficial relationships because by definition they would not go to the deep levels of my essence. They were safe relationships because I controlled them; I knew that I wouldn't get hurt because I wouldn't let them go deep. However, with Argyle and PJ, there was no real chance for growth or a meaningful exchange of emotions, but Dusty was different. Deep was the only place the relationship with Dusty could go and that scared me.

I, like most men I know, like to feel safe in relationships and for me, the only way to maintain safety was to create space between me and anyone who attempted to get close. I needed to control both my male and female relationships in order to ensure that I was safe and secure. Though even in this assumed net of safety, there appeared to be something missing. Reaching out was the only way to fill the void of what I thought was missing. But, just the thought of reaching out evoked feelings of anxiety, excitement, and fear. One thing for sure though, if I had to reach out to someone, Dusty seemed like the best person for me to grab. Best thing though, when I was ready to extend my hand and ask for help through some turbulent times, Dusty was there to lead me. He taught me to see things from a new perspective. He demanded that I start my exploration of things from within my own soul.

Dusty possessed a great deal of wisdom and after a while, something inside of me wanted just to be in his presence. He showed me places on the island that I would have never gone to see on my own. I gained a different perspective of the people that I once viewed simply as a resource to fill my personal desires. He pushed me to explore the barrios where the more traditional Filipinos lived and this proved to be an eye-opening experience.

I learned how they reverenced each family member and to see the manner of respect they held for their elders was humbling. They were deeply religious and community oriented. They never wanted to leave anyone behind; they progressed, grew, and prospered together. This was in complete contrast to the mannerisms and behaviors of most of the locals that I had grown accustomed to seeing just outside of the base. I learned that those closest to the base were just mimicking what they saw in the Americans they met even though it contradicted their own customs and beliefs. The pay we received while on the P. I. made us appear like people of wealth compared to the locals. We used the power of money to corrupt others and ourselves. Dusty knew that I needed to see the other side of the coin. He wanted me to think about what I was doing and how it affected others. I started to understand that just because you have the ability to do something does not make it right.

Dusty was trying to give me a sense of conscience. He had a nice apartment and even gave me a key. I felt like his son, but I was too embarrassed to tell him that I needed all of the attention and concern he showed me. Just like a son would do, I began to emulate the confident way he walked around and even began lifting weights in efforts to get big arms like Dusty. I wanted to tell him how much he meant to me but I could not find the words.

Ours was really like a father-son relationship. He supported me and I appreciated it. He came to my intramural basketball games. At one game, I was sitting on the bench and my friends were in the stands heckling me about why I was not in the game. Because being good in hoops was a big source of respect, on the bench wasn't the coolest place for me. The more they teased me, the angrier I got. I became so angry that I put on my sweats and started to leave the court. Before I could take three steps, Dusty came out of the bleachers and proceeded to read me the riot act. He told me that I would not embarrass myself by not finishing what I had started and that if I knew what was good for me, I'd take off my sweats and sit back down. I felt humiliated, but I knew that I had to respect him.

Later on, I realized I needed his firm hand to help keep me focused. I eventually got in the game that day, but afterwards my friends rode me even harder about how that old man went off on me. They clowned me and told me how I shouldn't have taken anything from him. I had to set them straight. I told them that they were wrong about Dusty and I was wrong for getting up. I believe I was starting to take baby steps in my development. The Bible says that "better is the ending of a thing than the beginning therof" and that's what Dusty was trying to teach me. He wanted me to be known as one who finishes what he starts and one who does not quit.

When Dusty would leave town on business, he trusted me to check on his apartment and pick up his mail. I found his place to be a nice place to bring a young lady when I wanted to try to impress her. One night I was at my best, or worst depending on your perspective, while trying to impress this woman. On one of my many romps about town, I came across a woman who was about 38 years old, now I was only 19 at this time. As a young man, I found some perverse sense of power by being with an older woman.

Maybe it was a teacher-pupil kind of thing, whatever it was; all I knew was that I was willing to be taught anything that this woman wanted to teach me. After much negotiation, I managed to convince a woman that her best bet was to spend the evening with me.

Well, who knew I'd get so lucky while Dusty was away? I needed a couple of items that were in my dorm room, so when we left the club, I asked the cab driver to take me by the dorms for a quick stop and then we'd be on our way. I guess the excitement of the moment and my relative inexperience took over so before I knew what was going on, I had done something pretty embarrassing. While the cab was rolling to a stop, I tried to jump out quickly to run to my room. Well, the cab had not completely stopped and when I exited the back seat, the rear tire rolled over my foot. Immediately, I lay down on the ground to keep my ankle from breaking. I yelled to the cab driver, "Back up! Back up!" The driver must have thought I was crazy. He looked at the woman and asked her "Are you sure you want to go with this guy?" She just looked at me and shook her head as if to say 'you need help.' I'm not sure which hurt more, my ankle or my ego. I felt like a fool lying on the ground with a taxicab on my leg. The driver eventually backed up and I hobbled to my room. Still on my mission, I picked up what I needed and made it back to the cab. The night pretty much went downhill from there. This was not what I would consider a smooth moment.

CHAPTER TWENTY-ONE
CAUTION: STUDENT DRIVER

There never seemed to be many dull moments as time went by in the P.I. and I was always in the middle of some interesting activities. Some were good and then some were not so good. Growing up in a big city had many advantages and one of them was public transportation. Everywhere I went in Stamford, or in New York, I could go by bus or train, so when I joined the military, I never had a driver's license. I had a limited amount of drivers training and that really did not work. My mother tried to take me out and teach me to drive; however, my mother was not exactly the most patient driving instructor and I wasn't the most polished student. Besides, it wasn't the coolest move around to have your mother teaching you to drive, so eventually we both just gave up. I couldn't ask my boys because that would just be too much to take from them. I knew that I was eventually going back to the states so I needed to learn to drive. I then did the unthinkable; I enrolled in driver's education while in the P.I. I tried to keep this a secret from my boys because I knew that this was one that I could never live down and I did a good job of not letting anyone know, but they found out on my job. One day my supervisor asked me to drop off some documents to the other side of base and said that I could take his car. I had to tell him the truth. He actually was the one who recommended that I take the class; he said his wife had taken the test and she was now a good driver.

The first day of class came and my instructor came out and shocked me. This guy looked like a throwback to the 1950s. He had a serious Elvis hairdo, with pork chop sideburns and all. Wearing these polyester pants with the wide waistband that made him look like he had won some type of wrestling championship. Those pants were way too tight and I often wondered if he could even find room in them for his driver's license. His shirt always was not fully buttoned and exposed part of his chest. I kept wondering who told this guy that this was the look that he needed to have. I was really starting to wish that somehow I had learned to drive before now because sitting through this with Dan Ramono as the instructor was going to be a real unique experience.

He was an American who had decided that his purpose in life was to teach drivers education in the Philippines. You couldn't tell this guy that he wasn't the coolest thing since sliced bread. In the middle of his teaching, he would always find a way to talk about himself and it really got old quick but I could not let on that his act was getting old because I needed to learn to drive. For the first week or so, we focused on classroom studies and he said we would soon be going on the road. I was the only male in the class and this did nothing for my ego. Every other student was a local girl that one of the guys had married and they wanted them to learn to drive. I was going every day after work and I was still able to keep this away from my boys, I was beginning to think that I could pull this off without any of them knowing. I would always find an excuse for not catching up to PJ and Argyle after work while I was in drivers' training.

The big day came in class when Dan Ramono told us that we would start doing some roadwork. I was excited because it meant that I was making some progress. The cars we would use were just like any other with a couple of exceptions: they had two steering wheels and brakes with the other set being on the passenger side. This was just in case there was a problem then Dan Ramono could take control. The part I found the most troubling was the giant sign that was on top of the car that read the same as the bright red letters on both the driver and passenger doors that simply stated ***CAUTION STUDENT DRIVER***.

I knew that this was not good for me. How could I remain anonymous during my training? Even to this day, when one of those cars passes by me, I look at the student driver and wonder if they feel like the loser I felt like. Grown men are supposed to know how to drive, right? All of the students were doing well on the road even though we were subjected to listening to rock and roll music all the time; that was what Dan loved. I was in my last couple of days and then I would be graduating with my international driving license; nothing could be better. I couldn't believe I was going to make it through this class without being found out, it was great. My exuberance was short lived.

The next day driving with Dan I saw a couple of my boys walking and I immediately began to feel nervous. They were having a conversation and did not see me coming and I hoped that it stayed that way. Well unfortunately, my luck ran out, they first spotted the neon sign on the car, and then they saw that it was me driving. I tried to look for the best in them and I said to myself that they would handle this with dignity and show me some support. They supported me by screaming, "Watch out there's a dangerous driver on the road." They then proceeded to dive into some bushes as if they were afraid that I was going to run them over. Dan Ramono asked me what that was all about and I said I had no idea why those guys were acting that way. As I looked back in my rear-view mirror, I saw them doubled over in laughter and knew that I was not close to hearing the last of this one.

They were all camped out by my room when I got back that evening and let me have it for what seemed like forever. I was a little embarrassed and angry but I think they drilled me harder because they said I should have told them in the beginning. In many ways, though it was cool because I didn't have the burden of hiding anymore. Eventually, I graduated and when they needed something dropped off on the other side of base, I was the first one to volunteer.

Another lesson was that not everyone with a driver's license could drive well. Even though I was qualified to drive, I still did not feel very comfortable with driving around. When I got back to the states, I found out that I had to take another test because they didn't honor my international license; but that's another story for later.

CHAPTER TWENTY-TWO
HARD KNOCKS

Someone once said that it is unfortunate that being young is wasted on the youth and that is true because we don't realize what we have. Physically we are at our best; we have opportunities and time to chase our desires. More times than not we don't exercise patience or understanding that often times comes from maturity and growth. Seeing only what we want and not fully examining all the attributes it will take to get to where we want to go. Not grasping the concept of the race; looking at it as a sprint versus a marathon. If things don't initially go our way then we just say that it probably wasn't the thing we needed to be involved in. I found myself the victim of my youth in a few instances and the results were not the best for me.

There was this girl named Tanya who was so fine that it was hard to decide if she looked better coming or going because both views were eye watering. She was about 5 foot 2 and weighed about 115 pounds. Her bowlegs made the curves of her hips seem even more pronounced. Mmmm, well-proportioned from top to bottom, Tanya demanded attention by her looks, as well as, her self-confidence, whenever she entered the room.

Everyone wanted to get next to her and I was definitely included in this group but at the same time, there was this girl named Linda who had expressed some interest in me. Linda was a high-quality woman who was a couple of years older than I was and she was extremely grounded in how she looked at life. Tanya on the other hand, was an outgoing wild child who I knew deep down could not be happy with staying with one man. I remember having some deep conversations with Linda about life and she did not just talk it, she walked it. Linda was, by most accounts, plain and unassuming in her appearance and demeanor. She always dressing conservatively, leaving more to the imagination versus flaunting her sexuality.

Linda was about 5 foot 5 and had a petite shape. Nothing really stood out about her on the surface, yet she seemed totally secure in who she was. She had gone out and purchased a house off base and whenever I saw her, she always seemed to be in the middle of doing something that was worthwhile for someone. I admired the way she put others before herself and she demonstrated something that was not common around the P.I., she had class about herself. When going out to the club, you'd see Tanya because she was the wild child but there was no way that you'd see Linda because she had figured out that there was nothing to be gained for her in that environment. Linda's ability to make others feel good about themselves was something that I considered a wonderful quality; she overlooked my current state of lack of focus and saw my potential. Eventually, Tanya and I hooked up and I could see that Linda was disappointed in my choice. Linda still would be there for me when I needed someone to talk to; she was a real friend and understood that being a friend sometimes meant loving someone even if you don't like the choices the person makes in life.

Tanya and I were having some good times but I noticed we had nothing in common other than the physical desire that raged in each of us. Linda and I had never been intimate but I felt much closer to her than I did to Tanya. This time, I was clearly caught up in the outside and missed the most important aspect — the heart. Dealing with Tanya was difficult because she was a free spirit and that meant that she was very open with herself to all. She would flirt but I didn't think she would take it any further than that, furthermore, I decided if I did not see her messing around then it did not exist. I started to notice her speaking to one of the guys that I played ball with from time to time. They called him Skid Row and he lived up to the nickname. He was as hard as they came on the court and off.

Row was about 6 foot 3 inches with a ripped physique, one of those brothers whose hands were so rough that you could strike a match in them. All he wore was white tee shirts, the kind mostly worn by people when they are arrested on television, I never saw him with a regular shirt on. You could tell he loved the name Row, and appeared to take his name literally, because he always looked like he needed a shave and a bath. I wondered what Tanya saw in him, he was just a roughneck who went around flexing on people. He had a reputation for using whatever means he deemed appropriate to get his point across; therefore, it was common for him to hit someone during a game if he had a disagreement. Most of the fellas tried to avoid Skid Row at all costs.

One night when the fellas and I were down town at a club, my choices in life once again caught up to me. Tanya and I were dancing and Skid Row walked up in the middle of us and started talking to her. I was totally caught off guard and asked him what he was doing. He told me if I knew what was good for me that I'd just step off. I must admit stepping off didn't seem like such a bad choice because I knew that Tanya really wasn't worth it; however, I couldn't allow Row to just chump me so, I told him that I didn't know what his issue was but it had nothing to do with me.

Before I knew what happened he was all over me. We were in the middle of the dance floor rolling on the ground. Once more, high school wrestling experience became a benefit. Although he was much bigger and stronger than I was, when we hit the floor, I had the advantage of leverage and center of gravity. I had him in a couple of knots, then I managed to look up, and I did not like what I was seeing. One of his partners was coming at me and I saw his fist heading towards my head. I knew that this was going to be bad, but at the last moment one of my boys caught him with a crushing blow to the head and then the whole club erupted. It seemed like a scene from a western movie; guys were running down the stairs with chairs hitting people over the backs. Meanwhile, I was doing my best to keep Row at bay and this was taking all that I had. I was hoping that someone would come in and break us apart because I was beginning to tire from all the tussling. I didn't know which was worse, actually fighting him or having to smell his stench as we rolled around. The chaos of the club spilled out into the streets and there were people fighting everywhere. The situation got so bad that the police showed up in riot gear and shot tear gas in the club. They were wielding their batons and using them with great precision. With that, Row and I let each other go, I straightened up my clothes and walked out of the club as if nothing happened. Many people were arrested that evening and I managed to slip out without being nabbed. The club was destroyed and they had to close it to make repairs.

The next day the fellas came around and said how messed up it was for Row to run up on me like that. I then felt like I could flex and started to say that he was lucky that we were broken up because I was about to finish him off. My mouth now was in overdrive. I harped that if I knew where he was; I would go and pick up where we left off. Well, one of my boys said they knew where he lived and that we should go to his house. This had clearly turned into another case of inserting one's foot in one's mouth.

So off we went to go over to Row's house, it just so happened that a friend of mine named Sam lived across the street from Row. The fellas all purchased some beer and meat and we had a barbecue before the action took place. I had to go and let Row know that I was there so, I went to his house. I could tell that he wanted some more of me and we walked out back to get it done. I really didn't want to fight anymore but once again, I got myself into this one.

Argyle was not there the previous night when we had fought and was extremely upset about him trying to jump on me. Argyle was pacing around like a caged animal and he let it be known that if it looked like things weren't going my way that he was going to even the situation. Row also had his boys there, but Argyle was the kind of guy no one wanted to tangle with. All of a sudden, Row said that he felt like the situation was not worth fighting over. I think it had less to do with me, Tanya, or the situation and more to do with Argyle. Phew, I managed to keep my manhood and face intact. From that point on, I never had anything else to do with Tanya.

It also seemed that Row had more respect for me and even when we played ball, he would not hassle me anymore. I became known as the dude who stood up to Row and lived to talk about it. In retrospect, if Linda were the person with whom I'd invested time; my life would have been much less turbulent. I felt bad about not being with Linda, feeling I had blown a great opportunity for something nice. When I ran into her later, I could see the disappointment in her face about me being caught up in mess behind Tanya. I simply told Linda she was right and I should have listened to her.

Linda again demonstrated her caring spirit by being kind to me even though I was running around like an out of control juvenile. She was not all glitz and glitter; however, she had an inner beauty that can only be appreciated by someone who possesses depth and vision and not focusing so much on sight. I wished I had taken the time really to look at her. Somewhere deep down I knew I had blown any chance of being with Linda only because I was walking around blindly following my sight and not my vision.

Enjoying Life at its Finest

ANOTHER SEASON

PHASE IV

CHAPTER TWENTY-THREE
PUSHED FORWARD

Clearly, in the P.I., behavior of the fellas was based on what they could see and this normally led to challenges. Most of us had never experienced free for all environments and without some guidance or intervention, the result would usually be being kicked out or worse.

The office I worked in had two brothers in the position I occupied before I had arrived and both of them were eventually booted. My section chief told me that I was not going to fail; he was tired of seeing young black males falling to the temptations of the P.I. He was also a brother, named Ron Sinclair, who knew the ropes inside and out. He and Dusty were friends, so if I weren't acting right then I'd have to get it from both angles.

I tried to keep most of my wild antics away from Sinclair and the rest of those I worked with. Somehow, I think Sinclair knew the deal about my wild activities but he never pressed me about what I was getting into down town. He would just say that if I did something stupid that he would apply some old school Air Force correction. He was a big fan of wall-to-wall counseling.

Sinclair was a big man with this deep baritone voice and when I was not doing the right things, I hated to hear him call my name. Standing about 6 foot 5 inches, with hands that swallowed mine every time we shook. He had caramel skin tone and looked well for what I assumed to be his age. In addition, he only had slight highlights of gray in his closely cropped hair. He had been in the P.I. for many years and was more of a native than anything else if you asked me. Any game that I was trying to run, he had already ran and perfected. It was clear that Sinclair had my best interest in mind. Sinclair would become a man that I would soon rely on during some turbulent times on my job.

During this time, my immediate supervisor was named Buford Renfro and he was a good old boy from Tupelo Mississippi. This guy was about 38 years old and had lost every tooth in his mouth that he was born with. The ones in his mouth stayed in a cup at night as he slept. He said that oral hygiene was not stressed in his family, and that he had a terrible appetite for chocolate as a child. A terrible combination for one's teeth and by the age of 15 he was a toothless wonder. The thing about having a mouth full of false teeth is that there was distinctive difference in his voice and pronunciation of words when he had his teeth in or out. When his teeth were out, he had trouble pronouncing words that ended with the letter k. Instead of saying desk, it would sound like "dest." Eventually I began to understand him. I preferred his teeth in because looking at his sucked in grill throughout the day was just too much for me.

Buford was a short and round fellow whose midsection seemed more dough than flesh. For the most part Buford tried to take care of me but he had a couple of shortcomings. One was that he was never around the office much and spent the time away either at home or somewhere drinking his favorite alcoholic beverage. I was left many times trying to take care of the functions in our office. I was beginning to hate being left because I knew eventually that someone would need something and I would not have a clue about how to take care of my customers. I made myself a vow that with or without Buford's help that I would find a way to become knowledgeable about my job and responsibilities. I would ask other troops around my organization and base questions to try to fill in my gaps of knowledge. Eventually, I managed to figure some things out and Buford did provide some help when he was around.

I was starting to get the hang of things around the office and didn't care if Buford was there or not. Confidence was starting to display itself and when people came by with a question or concern, they would leave with the right answer and quality administrative correspondence. However, one of Buford's other shortcomings would prove a problem to me and that was that he was not very strong in dealing with adversity. My training development manager was an old tobacco chewing, beer bellied, brown shoe, my way or the high way individual. Joe Sambrano for some reason did not take a shining to me, the new kid on the block, and this would soon lead to some challenging times.

Buford worked under Sambrano and Sinclair provided oversight over the entire directorate. It was Sambrano's job to make sure that each of the administrative specialists, which I was, were fully certified on required tasks and passed the written test needed to upgrade on the job. It soon became evident that upgrading would not be an easy task. It seemed like whatever I did was not good enough and Sambrano would find a reason to criticize what was being done by me. He would say that he didn't know how I made it this far, but if things did not change that I would not be a part of his Air Force anymore.

Several instances of public embarrassment took place when Sambrano was around. It almost seemed like he enjoyed yelling and saying how inadequate my progress was. I would talk to Buford and ask him to step in and stop the verbal abuse that I would receive from Sambrano, but all I would get from him was a shrug of the shoulders and he'd say that just hang in there.

I asked Buford why he allowed this to happen to me; it was the job of the supervisor to protect his troop and I needed some protection. Buford was afraid of anyone who outranked him, and in his eyes Sambrano was clearly his superior and one not to be challenged. Sambrano became worse and worse with me, he once said that he didn't like people like me and I wondered what he meant. I did not want to think that I was receiving all this grief because of my skin color. My lack of proficiency had less to do with my ability but more to do with his desire to see me fail.

One day during a routine training evaluation, I was decertified in training and placed in remedial training for not being able to perform a task for which I was never trained. When I told Sambrano that Buford and I had not gone over this procedure yet, he told me to quit making excuses. Buford was sitting right there and I asked Buford to verify what I said was correct and all he did was fidget with his false teeth. Decertification meant that I was one-step closer to being booted out of the Air Force if I could not meet the expectations of my trainer.

My training issues even affected my personal life because Sambrano said that while I was in remedial training that I could not participate in any extracurricular activities such as intramural sports or school. My initial upgrade training was supposed to be accomplished within one year. During that period, Sambrano said that I could not take off any days from work unless it was a national holiday.

I talked to some of my partners around the base and it appeared that I was the only one with such restrictions on me. I was wondering how much more of this I could take without exploding. Natural instincts can be a thing that can be good or bad, and my instincts were starting to kick in, because I am not one for being pushed to the wall.

I started to challenge Sambrano when he would talk to me in his indignant manner. I told him I was not going to take any more of his games and that it was people like him that I did not like. He seemed to like the conflict that he had created between the two of us; and I knew that Buford would provide no backup for me. I was starting to wonder what were the real reasons behind the two brothers before me being kicked out.

Seeing Sambrano win meant that I would have to lose and that meant my budding career would be short-circuited. Living with the thought that he wanted to see another career end was enough to make me hang in there. What would happen to the next young man that showed up that he didn't like. Would it just be more of the same? These answers were ones that I did not want to find out; I could not give him the satisfaction of quitting. However, he was in a key position to make it nearly impossible for me to succeed.

Sinclair was on the outside looking in, and he decided to take matters in his own hands. In his opinion, my work environment was not conducive to enhanced training so he decided that I would work for him. This meant I would not be under Buford anymore and he'd have to do his own work. All of a sudden, Buford wanted to speak on my behalf and say how much of an asset I was to our work section. Let's just say I didn't consider Buford an asset but a word that sounds like one. Buford would not be able to disappear anymore and have to earn his check.

Sinclair made it clear when Sambrano came around to take care of my certifications that there would be no games being played. Sinclair was hoping that Buford would stand up and take control of the situation and when he didn't and things were getting out of hand then he stepped in to intervene. Under Sinclair's watchful eye, I received a fair look as it related to training. All that anyone needs is a fair opportunity and finally it was happening for me. I was able to resume a normal life and Sinclair made sure that I got a day off here and there. Eventually, I was fully certified and ready to rock and roll.

As for Sambrano, his weight was always a challenging issue for him and it appears that someone made that known to our unit commander who took that very seriously. He was called in, put on the scale and the scale has not been the same since. Sambrano was not able to get his weight within standards and was forced to retire. No one ever found out who notified the commander about Sambrano, but I guess, all's well that ends well.

I clearly understood that a man is not to be judged by what he has but more importantly, by what he had to overcome to get it. Some people have things dropped into their laps. Never having to work for what they have in life. My training experience that I went through was difficult and frustrating at best, but through perseverance, I learned some valuable lessons. Even without having to deal with a nemesis like Sambrano, life is not going to be easy. There are going to be situations that arise that will make us ask ourselves if our dreams are realistic or reachable. That's when patience and perseverance will have to be at its peak because without them it will be difficult to keep going.

When I was at my breaking point in my training, I seriously contemplated giving up; wondering was going through all of this foolishness worth just being certified on my job. On the surface, the answer was an easy no. I mean there were many other occupations out there where I could work without having the pressure of someone standing on my neck and harassing me. Even when I was certified, there would be no fanfare or celebration because it was normal progression that all who had done this job before had to complete. Yet, for me there was a great sense of accomplishment because I knew how much Sambrano planned for me to fail. I felt proud that in the midst of the storm, I managed to hang on and eventually it passed.

I was happy I didn't quit, realizing that once you start quitting it becomes easier and easier as you go along in life. Our goals have to be greater than what is on the surface. We must view our challenges as stepping-stones and not stumbling blocks. That's why when I see someone who has an accomplishment I don't try to judge or value what they have done. Because if you don't know what it took for someone to overcome to get their achievement you may never understand why it means so much to them.

Many people had to put their hopes and dreams on the shelf while they took care of the necessities of life. Think of many people who decide to go to school later in life or pursue other desires once their children are out of the house. When you see these people walk across the stage to get their diploma, they often demonstrate an intense sense of accomplishment and pride. Yet, during that same ceremony, many others get the same recognition for the same accomplishment but they show no type of emotion. What is the difference? It is that some had to overcome greater challenges to get to the same place that others are. It goes back to vision because your vision will demand that you overcome the immediate inconvenience or setback to chase down the dream. Now that I overcame the latest challenge, I had a couple of choices: continue to focus on personal growth or resume my carefree behavior.

CHAPTER TWENTY-FOUR
A NEW AND DANGEROUS CREW

PJ, Argyle, and I were back running the streets again with regularity but for some reason I found a need for more and more excitement. I was afraid that if I weren't in the streets constantly that I would miss out on something. When the fellas didn't want to go out, I started to hang out by myself. This was very much out of character for me. I was usually the one who wanted someone around when I hung out and sometimes needed coaxing to do anything, but now; I was quite comfortable with running the streets alone.

I would go to places alone that I once felt nervous about going to with my friends. I saw many bad things happen to people in some of these places that I was hanging. I told myself that bad things happened to bad people or to those who are not wise to the fast life. That's how I convinced myself that I was fine when I was hanging in some of the shadier establishments around town. Eventually, I connected with a different crowd of people and these folks played for keeps. In this circle, it was common to see someone be bashed over the head with a bottle or stabbed over a minor disagreement.

With PJ, Argyle, and the other brothers I usually hung with, the worst that might happen was a scuffle, however the new crew I was running with was much more unpredictable. PJ and Argyle didn't even know about my double life with my new acquaintances. I knew they would disapprove and then ask me why I was putting myself in dangerous situations. If I could not figure it out for myself, then there was no way that I could explain it to someone else. My drinking was getting way out of control to the point where it started to affect the job.

It became harder and harder to get up in the morning and I was having to sometimes get a drink to steady myself. When I would hook up with PJ and Argyle they could not believe how much alcohol I was putting away. What they didn't know was that when they went in for the evening, I was moving on to phase two of my evening and assumed my alter ego. A friend of mine once said that when you fly with the flock eventually you have to spread your wings. Meaning that you had to take on the characteristics of the group you were with to fit in and I could see changes in me.

My late-night crowd consisted of some aggressive people who had no problem letting you know where they stood on an issue. If you did not share their point of view, then you had better be ready to defend your position. Many times, you had to defend your point by fighting. I found myself becoming more aggressive and things that I once feared now held no fear for me anymore. Surviving around a place where others became victims told me that I was not the hunted anymore but now I was the hunter.

I was out of control and running full speed on the road to self-destruction. The faces around me kept changing because people were being arrested, hurt, or worse; however, the situation never changed because there was always someone else who thought that they were above the results that others previously received. The first lie I told myself was that I had it under control, but it had me under control. I was just like an addict; the only difference was that my drug was my lust for the fast life. I told myself that I didn't have a need to go to the places that I went and since I knew that it was under control, then there was no reason to change my behavior.

Sinclair called me in his office one day and said that he was concerned about me. He stated he had a feeling that I was not taking care of myself. I thought that I was busted, afraid he had found out about my double life. He wondered if I had something on my mind that was causing me to lose focus and I told him that I was worried about my family at home. That could have been no further from the truth; I hadn't called home in months and had not really thought about my people back home. Looking back, it was crystal clear that I was a young man who was becoming someone that I didn't like. I stood there lying to someone I admired and respected. Someone who only wanted the best for me…this only made the situation worse. My mother did not raise a liar but that's what I had become.

Sinclair bought the story and offered his help if I needed anything. This only made me feel worse. He wanted the best for me and I was so ashamed that I had trouble even looking him in the face. I was now in a full sprint, running away from the things that could provide stability, dashing to things that could only lead to ruin. I thought I had it under control, if things got too bad then I'd just slow down. Running from me led to bigger issues because the world was waiting to take me in, gobble me up, and then spit me out with the rest of the garbage.

I was running but I could not figure from what. I loved PJ, Argyle, and had many others who cared about me like Dusty and Sinclair. All the love and support I needed was there but I had to reach out to accept what they had for me. My new set of acquaintances didn't care about me and deep down I wanted to believe that they were real and my true friends were the ones faking. For some reason, my thinking was so twisted that I thought that once again the ones who said they would be there would eventually walk away. I longed for true and deep meaningful relationships, and even though I had that, it seemed unrealistic. So, to preempt the letdown, I bailed from my friends and my mentors before they bailed from me. I felt just like that five-year old left struggling in the halls of that hospital, but instead of someone dropping me off, I jumped off into it on my own. Why was I replaying this situation? I knew Dusty and Sinclair were wondering what was going on in my head. I constantly tried to pray for God to give me the courage to reach out to them because I knew they loved me. It would have to be God because I did not have the strength to do it myself.

Part of me had no fear of death and would sometimes challenge death by inviting conflict with my aggressive behavior. I became known as the one you had better be ready to go the distance with if we tangled. One night my choice of lifestyle caught up to me. I was up to my usual habit of being in a place that I should not have been with someone I should not have been with when things went bad. While walking down a dark street on the way to a club, we were approached by several men. They were upset with the guy I was with and demanded that he pay some money they said he owed. I just wanted to get out of there, but I knew that I had better not make any sudden steps. I knew that they were packing and then one of them pulled out his gun. How could this be happening? I hardly knew this guy, and I definitely knew nothing about any money he owed.

There was no need to scream for help. Where we were, people didn't help you they just minded their business. I never imagined that when I died it would be in the middle of nowhere and for no apparent reason or that, I would be sharing the most crucial moment of my life with a guy who meant nothing to me. Yet, it was his activities affecting my life in a major way. Usually, I prided myself on always being ahead of things and not being caught off guard. As I looked around the alley, there appeared to be no realistic way to retreat.

I missed my opportunity to change my lifestyle and the cost was heavy. My life seemed like such a waste, so much promise, which now seemed like it was going to be unfulfilled. It's amazing what you think about when you face your mortality. Thoughts of family and maybe someday having a child passed through my mind. For some reason, I did not feel afraid anymore, I couldn't blame anyone because the choices that caused this to happen fell squarely in my lap. As I processed these thoughts, I was shaken from my internal conversation by hearing the guy plead vehemently for more time to pay his debt.

I could hear the fear in his voice and see the desperation in his eyes. The guys with the guns seemed very anxious and started to discuss what to do with the two of us. Having a gun and being anxious are not two things that you want to say about someone holding you at bay. Finally, they approached me and said that I could go because they had no business with me. I could not believe what I was hearing but did not stay around for them to clarify any further. Part of me felt bad for leaving, but I didn't know what else to do. I literally felt like I dodged a bullet. I went straight home and thanked God for sparing my life. I then knew that I had to make some changes and explain my behavior to my real friends.

Living on the Edge: Running Fast and Furiously

CHAPTER TWENTY-FIVE
MENDING FENCES

PJ had taken leave to go home and that left Argyle and I to hold it down on our end until his return. I wanted to have them both together when the subject of my wild side would be discussed so PJ's absence bought me some time. There was no need to tell this story twice and to be honest; I didn't look forward to telling it once. Argyle and I seemed to get much closer during PJ's time at home. We had conversations that are more candid. He confessed how deeply he cared about Marisol and how much it hurt him when she cheated with PJ. Even though he appeared to be himself and attempted to move on, a part of him had not recovered from the pain of losing her. Argyle said that he tried to stay busy in athletics, other women, or any activity that would keep his mind off the pain of not having her in his life anymore.

I always saw Argyle as an invincible young man who was as tough as they came. In the midst of our surface relationship, I missed many signs of his needs and insecurities. He told me that everyone has always seen him as a strong person who had everything under control. His parents had money and lavished him with whatever he wanted, but there were things that he said he needed at home that he never received.

He told me that he felt like he could never gain the acceptance of his father when he was at home. Even though he had done well in school as a child, in his mind it never met the high expectations of his father. His mother was supportive, but retreated when his father would start in on him about not living up to his potential. A lifetime of issues, culminating with losing Marisol, came to a head during our conversations. She was the one person who accepted Argyle for who he was and cared for him.

Right before my eyes, he began to cry and say how much of a lie his life had been. That he only used his talents and gifts to pacify those around him, to deflect the attention from his inner yearnings to be accepted. Being the center of attention had weighed heavily on him and he was growing weary of being the man, when all he wanted was to grow into a man. He was sobbing uncontrollably at this point and I remember a deep feeling of being helpless. How could I have missed his despair and cry for love. He just sat there on the floor of my dorm room against my wall locker with this distant look on his face. I couldn't find any words to say, none seemed adequate, I sat there next to him in silence for what seemed like eternity. It was the very first time I saw him for who he was, a scared and insecure young man. On the inside, he felt much the same as I did.

He told me that he didn't want to be alone that night and asked if he could stay in my room. I knew his pain, I knew how it felt to be surrounded by people your entire life, yet live in solitude. In the midst of all of the fanfare and people, Argyle was a lonely man. He, too, was lost among the throngs of people in his life. I didn't know what to say. I reassured him that I loved him and I hugged him. Uncle Robert taught me that. Then both of us cried for what seemed like forever. I just wanted him to know that it didn't matter to me what he did in life because I just loved him for who he was.

After that, Argyle said that he missed me and was worried about where I was during many of my unexcused absences from him and PJ. Now the spotlight was on me and this made me feel even worse because I'd just realized that when I thought I was only hurting myself while running the streets, I was also hurting my friends. I had allowed my own desires to take me away from those who I cared for the most, but I felt good because I was now being given another chance to be a friend to Argyle.

Eventually PJ came back from leave and once again, the trio was back together. We all sat down to recap what had taken place since our last time together and there was one major surprise. PJ told us that he and his high school sweetheart were hanging tough when he was home and they were hooking up again like old times. We really were not surprised by that but when he said that she was pregnant, Argyle and I were floored. PJ was hyped about being a father and I didn't know what to think. I never thought that he would show such enthusiasm about being a father, but he said he always wanted to be one.

Argyle and I promised that if there were ever a need, we would be there for his child. I saw a change come over PJ; he started to talk about his future and the future of his child. He said that he wanted to demonstrate how important an education is and started to focus on college and other technical certifications. I was proud of him and tried to encourage him as much as I could. We were all maturing in our own way.

Finally, I told them all about my activities when I was running the streets solo. I laid it out and I was ashamed to tell them some of what I was doing but I knew that I had to because I needed a cleansing. They were shocked by what they were hearing and their looks made me feel even worse. When I finished, they just embraced me and said that they were happy that I had come back to my senses. Both of them let me know that it didn't matter what I had done, they were just happy that I was back with them. They stressed that I could bring anything I was going through to them and they would not judge me. As far as they were concerned, what I had done was in the past and they said we never had to discuss it again. I was grateful for their unconditional love and acceptance. I realized that I had nothing to fear and hoped that if put in their shoes that I could respond the same way.

That day we came into a new level of friendship, we left agreeing that we would accept and not judge the choices we made or will make in our lives. None of us ever looked at the other the same after that day. A lot happened in this brief time we spent together: I nearly lost my life, Argyle began to find his, and PJ helped to create one.

We were all embroiled in the school of hard knocks; somehow, through all of this, I felt that I was maturing. Although my road was much bumpier than others were, I was just happy to still be standing and facing my issues instead of running from them.

After getting back into the fold with my two dear friends, I still had some fence mending to do. Dusty and Sinclair were both heavy on my heels about my erratic behavior and for the most part, I had managed to keep them at bay. But, while I was out with Argyle and PJ one night, we ran into the two of them in a local lounge. Argyle and PJ knew what I was in for, so they did as any good friend would do: they left me to take my brow beating alone while they shot pool.

The thing about it was that Dusty and Sinclair approached me in a nice enough manner. They never mentioned to me that they knew what I was doing and with whom, even though I knew they had to know. They just said that are not going to sit by and allow me to destroy myself and that I had more sense than that. Simply stated, I knew better. Sinclair asked, "Boy, when was the last time you talked to your mother?" He knew that she meant a lot to me but I had to confess that I had not talked to her much lately. He really hit below the belt with that one and I felt like I was getting smaller by the minute.

Guilt had the better part of my conscious and I had trouble looking them in the eye. I had let down the two people I admired the most. They kept saying to me, "Look at us when we're talking to you!" Well, they weren't just saying it; you know they were practically yelling it. I looked to PJ and Argyle for help but they acted as if they were into their game. I knew they wanted no part of this conversation and I could not blame them. Man, I felt like the prodigal son who had left home, disappointed his father, and wanted so dearly to come home but shame kept him away. When I did, or could look into their eyes, I didn't see anger or frustration; all I saw was concern and love. The father was hurt that his son was away and doing dangerous things, but he never stopped loving his son. I was ready to come home but was afraid of being ridiculed and rejected. However, it became much easier when I saw Dusty and Sinclair's eyes. They knew that I was not safe, like the father in the story; all they wanted was for the son to come back to reality.

Dusty and Sinclair were not even concerned about what I had been doing or with whom; they just wanted to be the ones who helped to mold me, who helped to bring me back to myself. I never wanted to let them down again and vowed to do better about the choices I made in life. I knew that I could share anything with them and they would be there. Once they finished with me, they pulled in PJ and Argyle and reminded them what friends are supposed to do for one another and that we were not doing enough to support each other. They were right but what they didn't know was that we had discussed this and were committed to each other in a new and real way. Now that things starting to stabilize for me, I had another change introduced into my life, I was going on my first temporary duty.

CHAPTER TWENTY-SIX
HEADACHE & HEARTBREAK IN KOREA

The runway on the P.I. was being repaired and our aircrafts were going to be sent to Japan and Korea while all modifications were implemented. Since I supported those who flew, I had to go to one of these locations for a couple of months. I was not excited about going to either place because each location was so unfamiliar to me and I've always had trouble being alone in unfamiliar places. But, they soon told me that my duty would be in Osan, Korea and that I had better get my bags packed.

I told PJ and Argyle that I would be leaving in about another week and they suggested that we kick it hard before I left. So, we all hung out and had some good times together. Sinclair and Dusty sat me down and told me what to avoid and I knew that I did not want to let them down. I was going to be in charge of the mailroom for over 700 people and I knew nothing about setting up a mailroom and managing thousands of pieces of correspondence. I was going to this place with a bunch of people and I did not know one of them, man, I didn't even know who was going to be my new boss. Once again, I started to feel alone.

I tried to look at the bright side. The flight over was only a few hours and I thought for sure that Korea was similar to the P.I., so, it should not be much of a transition. We flew over on a C-130 cargo plane, which is not a smooth ride. Heck, this plane was built to haul equipment and combat troops. It took many dips and turns that it felt like a roller coaster. I prayed that I did not lose my lunch, so when the pilot said we were landing I was relieved.

Once the cargo doors opened, I realized that this was not the P.I. First, when we got on the plane in the P.I. the temperature was about 85 degrees, but in Korea in February the average temperature is about 20 degrees, it was bitterly cold, and snow was everywhere. We had to off load all of our bags and equipment to set up operation in this new land and that was a great deal of work. I couldn't decide which worse, the bitter wind and cold or the heavy lifting. As an administrative specialist, I was not accustomed to manual labor, I just wanted to get something to eat, take a shower, and get some rest.

After all, that hard work and driving around the base for the longest time, we pulled up in front of a series of tents. This clearly was a mistake because we had to be staying somewhere else and I wondered who would have to stay in these tents; then they ordered us to get off the bus. This was not working out at all; in fact, it was going downhill fast and I wondered if I'd have fared out better if I'd selected Japan instead. On top of everything, it started to snow!

This place looked more like a refugee camp than a military base and I felt like someone on a camping trip that had gone very bad. To ease my frustration, I went to the gym to play some ball and met a few cool fellas along the way. One guy, Keith, was actually stationed in Osan and lived in the dorms. I told him about my dilemma and he said that I could sleep on the floor of his room and I was more than happy to do that. This seemed like a good plan and I was pleased with being in a heated room with a real shower down the hall. Keith's roommate worked a swing shift and I could tell that he was surprised to see me lying in the floor when he got off work. He seemed cool about it and didn't put up much of a fuss.

After a couple of days, some of the fellas in tent city started to ask where I had been. I told them of my set up in the dorms and before you knew it, we had quite a few fellas taking up residence in all kind of places. Keith's roommate had enough out of us, and told his First Sergeant, who in turn contacted our First Sergeant. Well, the party was over and we all were back in tent-city before we knew what happened. I knew I should have quit while I was ahead.

Going back to the tent again was a major downer and I was looking for something to make me feel better. In the life of a man, few things can make him feel better than the support of a woman. I was about half way through my tour overseas and knew the day would come when I would return to the states and it was time to make sure that there would be a warm reception upon my return. I had been writing Jenny on a regular basis while I was in the P.I. and would call her from time to time as well. We wrote about getting together after my return but I'm not sure how serious either one of us really were. It's funny about when you are lonely how things can start to look differently to you. In the P.I., the focus was never on any girl in particular because there were so many to choose from; when one didn't act right then you'd just slide to another one. This was just the environment that existed over there. Korea was very different because I had no established routine or network of women. So, the first person that came to mind was Jenny because she represented stability and acceptance, it wasn't even about sex for me. I knew that if I heard her voice and talked to her that I would feel better about being in this place.

I scraped some money together and went to the recreation center where you could make overseas calls back to the states. I finally reached Jenny and began to talk to her about my experiences in Korea. She began to question me about why I had not been staying in touch as much as she liked. I was thinking that she would be happy just to hear from me but I was clearly wrong on all accounts. I asked her what was wrong, but then the overseas operator said I needed more money to continue the phone call. I began to deposit more. It seemed like every time we got to a point in the conversation where she was about to tell me what was bothering her, the operator would then ask for money. How could a girl who wrote in the high school yearbook that her future goal was to become Mrs. "B" act so distant and cold.

Had I lost some of the appeal that she once saw in me, this was not going as planned.

When I had finally loaded up a good chunk of money to the operator, again I soon began to wish that I wasn't hearing what she was saying. Jenny said that she needed the same thing that I had called her for, support and reassurance. Unfortunately, she never received either from me while I was gone. A part of me understood that she patiently waited for me to demonstrate something to her, anything. She told me that she had found someone who could fulfill her needs in a real way. Being a young man who did not understand the things that it took to satisfy a woman, I took her statement to mean that she had physical needs that were being met better than I could. I was way off.

My conversation with Jenny was not going as planned and I hoped the operator would hurry up and just cut the line. Once again, I felt lost and alone again after talking to Jenny. I respected what she said and understood that she did deserve better. A part of me hoped that she received her heart's desire; I just didn't want to know about it anytime soon. She let me down easy and even left the door open if, in her words, I began to take her love seriously. To begin with, the entire nature of my phone call was selfish. I only wanted to be comforted and really was not concerned with Jenny in a healthy way. Attempting to do a better job of staying in contact with my mother, I began to call home more. She would ask me what I was doing and of course, like any good son, I would provide the G-rated version of my life. Then the inevitable question, "Have you been going to church?" I offered one lame excuse after another and then tried to change the subject.

For my family, church was something that was a constant and I had no reason for shunning a part of me that was the most important, my soul. Figuring like most that there would always be plenty of time to get things right with God, I continued to forsake God in my life and focused on the thrill of the moment versus my eternal destination. Was I running from God? My mother never pressured me about not going to church but clearly, this was something that bothered her. She was just happy to be hearing from me again on a regular basis and it was through this period that our bond began to get deeper.

Another weekend had fallen upon us and as usual, it was time to go on the town and kick it again. Downtown was an environment that was hectic and full of many places to satisfy your every desire. As soon as you left the gate, you were confronted with vendors offering up everything from jewelry, food, clothing, and even sex. There were all kinds of clubs that catered to whatever you wanted. Primarily, I went to the R&B spots to see what the scene was like. One night when I was out, I saw someone that made things better.

I thought I noticed a face that looked like someone I knew. It couldn't be, could it? This person was talking to a young lady at a corner booth, so I moved in to get a closer look. As I closed in it became evident that the person talking to this young lady was PJ. I ran over and he saw me before I could reach him and met me in the middle of the dance floor. All of a sudden, Korea did not seem bad anymore; everything seemed like it was going to be fine. PJ had to come over to Korea because another person in his shop became ill and could not travel. He did not know how to get in touch with me when he arrived but figured that eventually I would show up at the club. Now, it seemed warmer outside; not something that could be noticed by a temperature reading but things definitely were becoming more pleasant. We caught up on all of the happenings since I had left to go to Korea.

One of the coolest experiences to have is to be in a foreign country with a friend. PJ and I had shared many moments together in the Philippines, but that's the place we met. I can't explain how it felt to go to an entirely different country and experience new things together. That's one of the cool things about being in the military. We made a promise to each other that for the rest of our lives we would meet from time to time to catch up on life. It did not matter where we were, or what our life situations were; we felt that we owed that to each other. We couldn't wait to tell Argyle of our pact and have him join in it as well when we got back to the Philippines.

PJ worked in Information Technology and gave me a tour of his work area while we were in Korea. A couple of things jumped out to me during my tour of his facility. First, PJ was much more intelligent than I had given him credit for because as he explained his responsibilities it became evident that he not only was very knowledgeable about his job but also was very proficient. The other people in his section seemed very pleased with his performance and several high-ranking people commented about how skilled he was. I was proud of him and I think he enjoyed showing me how much he knew about the automated systems he was required to maintain and service.

I decided to be a better friend to PJ and stop missing his true qualities. I wanted to know the things that were important to him. His biggest focus was the child that he had on the way and what kind of a father he would be. PJ was determined to go to school and set himself and his child up for a successful future. With PJ alongside, the remaining months in Korea flew by and before I knew it, I was back on my way to the Philippines. PJ left a couple of days after me and our trio was back in effect again.

  I managed to function well on the job while in Korea. All reports to Sinclair gave good feedback on my performance and he made sure to let me know that he was proud. He hadn't heard about my dormitory issues, because of the old

Air Force adage, "what happened TDY stayed TDY."

CHAPTER TWENTY-SEVEN
CHANGING TOURS

PJ, Argyle, and I had been in the P.I. about the same amount of time and we all had choices we had to make about our next assignments in the Air Force. The choices we all would make would change our lives in ways that none of us could imagine. The chance of the three of us being assigned together again was slim so we didn't even entertain that concept much at all. It was something that we didn't discuss because the idea of the three of us being separated was something that did not seem natural. Argyle agreed to meet us from time to time wherever we were in the world.

I came up with the bright idea that we all could extend in the Philippines and our time together would go on for times to come. I had figured it all out and the three of us would be chillin' like old times again. However, with all good plans there were a couple of factors beyond my control. First, when this brilliant proposition was presented to Sinclair, he didn't buy it. You see, Sinclair had to recommend approval for anyone in his chain of command to be able to extend in the P.I. Sinclair said that there was no way that he could support me staying there one more day than was scheduled. His thinking was that it was for my own good and going to a slower and structured environment was the best thing possible. As usual, he was correct but how many people like to hear what they need versus hearing what they want. The other sticking point, PJ was excited about being in the states for his baby. Argyle was ready to stay but given the fact that the two of us had to leave for different reasons, he resigned himself to going back to the USA.

Finally, the day came when assignments started to roll in and I was the first to find out my next place of residence for the future. Shaw Air Force Base,

South Carolina was the destination for me. I had never been in SC and the prospects of being in the Deep South seemed to be unsettling. I wondered how many Sambranos I'd have to deal with; you know the type, people who don't like you because of what you look like or where you come from, or in some cases for reasons that you may never find out, but you just know that whatever you do will never be good enough for people like this.

Instead of focusing on what would happen in the next few months in SC, I decided to enjoy the time that was left in the P.I. Many hours have been wasted on worrying about what might happen and ending up missing what's happening. I hoped that PJ and Argyle would be nearby and that would make things much more manageable. My hope was short lived because when I got together with the two of them, they made me aware of their next assignment. Argyle would be going to Las Vegas, NV and PJ was going to Phoenix, AZ. They were both in two nice locations with many things going on and I was still trying to find where Sumter, SC was on the map.

Oh, they rubbed it in, talking about how easy it was going to be for the two of them to meet up and do things together and I knew that there was no way I could be there. I might as well have been on the other side of the world because I was on the opposite side of the United States in relation to them and my opportunities to see them would be slim.

Time was really starting to draw near for our departure back to the states and I would be the first one to head back. It was becoming more and more difficult to focus on what lay ahead because to move on to the next phase that requires closing a chapter and turning to a new page. Once again having to say goodbye to those who became an important part of my life was looming ahead. People always say that they are going to stay in touch, but how many really do. I prayed that my departure would not be a series of goodbyes but instead until we meet again.

Dusty and I were spending more time together; I guess he was trying to give me all that he had before I left. When we would talk, he would express himself with a deeper sense of urgency in regards to decisions I would have to make in life. A constant theme for him was that I was given an opportunity that many before me had not been afforded.

One day he took me on a long drive and for the duration of the drive, he was silent; he seemed almost in another place so I chose not to disturb him with idle conversation. We drove for a couple of hours through winding roads and began to ascend upward towards the once distant mountains. Finally, we reached the crest of this green mountain in a remote part of the island. It was a beautiful place to see. A tropical mountain paradise surrounded by rich and beautiful flowers. I immediately noticed how much cooler it was at this elevation as opposed to where we had come from, but it felt great.

I figured that Dusty must have had his reasons for this trip so I decided to wait for him to talk. He motioned that I should follow him and we began to walk through a winding trail. This was more bushes and thickets than trail or path and looked like no one had ever ventured this way before, it was rough going for a while and we had to be careful of what steps we took because the footing was loose in some areas. I wished that I had worn sweat pants because my legs had a few scrapes on them from some of the bushes we walked through.

Dusty continued to walk and I tried my best keep up with him. He didn't even look back; he just kept going so I pressed on to keep pace with him. Eventually, we came to a clearing where in the midst was a waterfall, which created a soft mist, spraying its moisture upon my face. After all, of our hiking, the mist was a welcome relief and I began to feel rejuvenated. I noticed this place was even more pristine than the place that we had left the car. It seemed like God, Himself, handcrafted this spot and I felt privileged and humbled at the same time. There were flowers there that I had never seen before and tropical birds of magnificent color, singing wonderful songs of joy. I closed my eyes and just listened for a while to the chorus of the birds and allowed the air and the mist to comfort me. There was a sense of power, which came from the crashing water at the bottom of the waterfall. A delicate fragrance was evident from the mountain flowers, which carpeted the clearing where we stood.

I felt upset that I did not have a camera to capture this rare sight of God's radiance but soon realized that a picture would not do this any justice. Realizing that some things are better maintained in one's heart and soul, and this was something that I would never forget. For a while, it seemed like there was no one around, I had forgotten that Dusty was even there. Finally, I opened my eyes and noticed Dusty sitting on a stump and I joined him.

After a few minutes more of silence, he began talking about his views on life and how what he valued had changed over the years. He stressed that life is about making adjustments and changes at different points. Dusty said that now he understood that living with change is difficult because it involves taking a sincere look at who we are, but he also knew that it was impossible to live without change. He wanted to prepare me for the different life stages that I would face.

Dusty told me that for most of his life he got by on his charisma and charm, because he was well liked, many of his indiscretions were overlooked. He said that one day he looked within and saw a man not living up to his potential, not from a professional standpoint but as being a man of character. Dusty did not want to be remembered as one of those who said one thing and did another. He said a few years back there would be no way that he could have this conversation with me because he was not being real within himself. He thanked God for allowing him to wake up on his own and not due to some major traumatic event in his life.

Dusty said that he saw many of his characteristics and talents in me, and I remember feeling proud because this man meant everything to me. I would have walked through fire for him and to think that he saw in me promise and potential was incredible. Dusty said that I could be my best proponent or worst enemy depending on the choices I made in life. His belief, which I shared, is that talent can take you places but you can only stay there if you have character. Talent can come and go but character is there for a lifetime. Dusty said it was time for me to be a man of character. He defined character as doing the right thing when no one is looking. I did a quick mental inventory, did not like what I came up with, and began to feel ashamed. My face must have shown it because he said that he was not judging me or disappointed; he just wanted me to know how much he loved me and that it was extremely important to him that I did not repeat the same mistakes that he made earlier in life.

There was no concern of the things that I had done in the past; he wanted the focus to be on the future. Dusty never had any children and said that he regretted not having someone to pass his values and wisdom to and he felt that I was placed in his life to mold and refine for the journey ahead. His eyes were welling up with tears as he continued to do all he could to usher me from a child to a man. He then gave me a gift that I could never repay but have spent the rest of my life trying. He said, "No matter what you have done or gone through I am proud to call you my son." He actually saw me as his son.

Those words caused emotions to reach a point of overflow within my spirit. Still silent, I began to choke back tears that were at the surface. He began to say that he wished that he had something to give me to be able to remember our time together and now I know he did give me something that I would always cherish. That day, Dusty's gift to me was unconditional love. That kind doesn't ask why or point an accusing finger. It loves just because, in spite of whom we are. For the first time I felt like a son who had a father who cared for me.

I was speechless and continued to listen as attentively as I could because somewhere deep inside I knew that once we left this place, we would have to return to our lives. But, for now, we were immune from all the influences of the world and the uncertainty, which loomed ahead in a new place for me. I did not want to leave this place. Not because of the immaculate beauty, which the eye beheld, it was much deeper and beautiful than what the naked eye could see. It was two people who shared an experience only realized through freedom of spirit and genuine trust and there was nothing that could come between the two of us.

We had arrived in a place that few get to experience and for that, I will be eternally grateful. Then came a moment that I dreaded; I knew that it was time for us to leave. Dusty stood up and I joined him by his side trying to comprehend what had just happened. My eyes now full of love and tears, afraid that if I tried to speak that I would break down, Dusty put his arms on my shoulders and looked at me with deep sincerity and simply said, "It's time for you to be the man you are destined to be." He gave me a powerful hug and I felt like a child who was leaving home for the first time.

I didn't want him to release me, I felt scared and safe at the same time. After he released me, he simply turned and headed back towards the way we entered. I walked behind him towards the car, but I had to turn and look back at the place where I received one of the most profound life lessons that I would ever experience. As the sun continued to descend, there was a feeling that a chapter of life would be closing. While we walked, I was already missing Dusty.

Even though he gave me so much during this day, a part of me felt sad because I knew that I would not be around Dusty anymore and I was starting to feel how much this man meant to me. The ride back was as quiet as the one there. What more needed to be said or expressed? Dusty dropped me off at my dorm and I still had not said a word the entire time. Somehow, I knew that he understood what I was feeling; I simply waved to him and walked up to my room. That night I smiled through my tears because I knew that as long as I held on to what Dusty challenged me to be that I would carry him with me wherever I went. Dusty understood the power of one and the concept of unity. He taught me that knowledge and wisdom are not to be kept to ourselves but should be shared and searched for like precious jewels.

Life's experiences and lessons are invaluable and being focused on oneness allows us to all benefit from the testimonies of each other. Dusty was committed to contributing to a promising future to whoever would listen to him and I for one hoped to be in a position one day to be able to continue that tradition by pouring into someone else.

CHAPTER TWENTY-EIGHT
THINGS MUST CHANGE

Now, there was one day was left before I finally left to return to the states and I had done all my packing. The only thing that remained was the last night on the town with the fellas and I would be heading back stateside. PJ and Argyle did a great job of keeping whatever they were planning a secret from me and I gave up on trying to find out what it was. The two of them came by my room to pick me up for what I expected to be an interesting night. I made sure to have all my bags packed before we left because there was no telling what time I would get home.

First stop: they took me to the Airman's Club on base and the three of us sat down for a nice meal. Already, this was starting out to be bitter sweet because many of our best moments came at the Airman's Club and just knowing that this was our last time there as a trio tore at my heart. We planned to make this evening like all the others we had shared together, full of fun and laughter, not focusing on the finality it represented. Inevitably, the discussion started to become a reflection of how the three of us had become one. We admired the way petty envy turned into genuine admiration for the different talents each one of us possessed. PJ and Argyle teased me about how I was the only guy walking around the base with a Shag haircut and how long it took them to convince me to finally cut it. Dinner was great and afterwards we shared a toast pledging our commitment to one another for times to come. PJ, Argyle, and I sat there for a few moments in awkward silence not knowing what to say or do next. This was really beginning to hit home; I am really leaving my friends and this place.

The look on the faces of PJ and Argyle told me they were dwelling on the same thing I was. The waitress came up and asked if we were ready for the check and her presence snapped us out of our funk. They then said it was time press on with the rest of the evening.

Second Stop: a cab ride later, we were downtown heading to one of our favorite hangouts called The Third Eye. Once inside I was greeted by many of my acquaintances, there was cake, and other party items and it dawned on me that they were all there for me. Even Dusty and Sinclair came out to support me one last time. It excited me to see them because this place was not Dusty's or Sinclair's cup of tea, yet they saw fit to be there. Seeing them meant a great deal to me and I was starting to feel a flood of emotions.

Again, I managed to fight back the feeling to break down and focused on the party at hand. There was the cutting of the cake and several toasts made, the evening was now in full swing. PJ and Argyle said we had a traveling party and it was time to go to the next location. The clubs downtown were all within walking distance of each other and it appeared that we'd be making the rounds this evening. Dusty and Sinclair said their good-byes and for the party to go on without them. Before our procession headed out of the club, I focused on Dusty and Sinclair for a moment. Together the two of them had played tremendous roles in my development and planted seeds, which would later blossom into better things. At least that was their hope and mine as well. They both raised their glasses and toasted me as I moved towards the door. I felt my throat tighten up and I swallowed to fight back the tears. By this time, my entourage ushered me out the door and I simply waved farewell to my two mentors as we took our evening to the streets.

Third, Fourth and Fifth Stops: our entourage had grown considerably and behind PJ, Argyle and I were over 40 people. We went from club to club partaking of the flavor of the day in each one. After about the eighth establishment, I felt little or no pain. The We Funk Crew was in full effect, and in one club, we put on a show for old time's sake.

We danced, sang, and got on the microphone and I rapped until sweat was pouring off me. By this time, my sweat was probably 80 proof due to the amount of celebrating we'd already done. If I was going to make it through the night, I was going to have to pace myself, but everyone was trying to buy me a drink and there was no way that I could keep up with the amount that continued to flow my way. I started to give my drinks away or find skillful ways to slide them away from me.

Of course, when you are about to leave and you introduce alcohol in the equation; people begin to be candid about whatever is on their mind. I often heard the saying "a drunk man speaks with a sober tongue." Everyone has a strong opinion on whatever you are talking about when he's drinking. I cannot count the number of testimonials that were given that evening about any and everything that you can imagine.

The one thing that had me scratching my head was the number of women who expressed their attraction for me and related how they regretted that we never spent any time together. Some of these women were ones that I would have loved to hook-up with, but due to the fact I was running so hard, I guess that I missed some of the opportunities that were right in front of me. Shoot, it would have been better if these women had not said anything at all about their attraction because there was no way anything was going to happen on my last night. My female friends tell me that women drop subtle hints to let a man know of their interest; however, it is important for them to know if the man is astute enough to notice these signals. If the targeted man is not quick on catching signals, then he may end up like I did on my last night: receiving testimonials from women who said they wish they had more time. Honestly, more time wouldn't have made a difference because more than likely, I still would have been missed their signals. PJ and Argyle were right on time and interrupted another "we could have been…" conversation with another young lady and we were off to another location.

The processional had really grown and it was futile even to try to count how many were in our group. Each club we entered drew smiles from the club owners because we immediately filled the establishment with our festive group. My head was spinning and I began to hope that my plane would leave the next day because I couldn't endure another night like this. It was hard to comprehend how one person could receive so much love and generate so much emotion. I was the first one of our group to leave and all of us realized that things would not be the same anymore and the presence of all my friends spoke that in a loud voice.

It was about 1 am and we were still going strong, I recall going down the street riding the shoulders of the throng. It seemed like the party would never end, but it had to because show time at the flight terminal was at 0700. Of course, towards the end of the night, everyone wanted to toast again and this was putting icing on top of the cake. The last thing any of us needed was another toast or two but we complied anyway.

With the help of a patient and friendly cab driver, I made it back to the dormitory for what now would be a quick nap and then off to the airport. Thank goodness, I had the foresight to set the alarm clock before we went out. I didn't recall falling off to sleep and my rest came to an abrupt halt with PJ shaking me awake and I could hear my alarm clock blaring in the background. It had been going off for a while and I had never heard a thing.

PJ had a feeling that I would have a problem getting up and came by my room to check. Now see, PJ was loyal to the end.

I had 15 minutes to get to the terminal to meet my aircraft. If it had not been for him, I would have missed my plane. When I got to the terminal, a few of the fellas who could muster up the strength to get up were there to send me off in style. Argyle was passed out in his room, I expected that because of the amount he drank the night before. In some ways, it was good that I was running late because I didn't have to go through the awkward moments of leaving at the terminal.

I checked my bags in and had only a moment to say farewell. The people around us looked at us funny and I didn't know why until I thought about it. We all looked like we were coming off a three-day drunk and smelled the part as well. A couple of my boys shedding tears and I guess we were a pathetic sight to see. I did my best to hold it together because I didn't want to cry in front of all those people. I was doing well until I embraced PJ; it was different with us, we were brothers. I couldn't believe that I would not see him later that day after work like I always did. Thoughts and memories of our times together began to flood my mind and I felt a deep sadness.

We just stood there in the middle of the terminal holding on to each other, not wanting to let go. I just held on until I heard the attendant say it was time to board. I wanted to speak but what was there to say. Sometimes the words just get in the way. As I walked to get on the plane, I looked and saw all of my partners embracing themselves as if to pull together. I loved thinking that the fellas would stick together and I felt jealous because for the first time in a long time I had no one to hold on to and no one there to get my back when I needed it.

I had been running full speed in life, surrounded by many people, and having experienced more than a poor little boy from Connecticut could have wished. In the end, I was alone, again. It was time to stop running and face what life had to offer. I couldn't run from myself anymore.

Floods of thoughts began to run through my mind. I could see prominent people from my past that had their heads on straight such as Cuda and Jake. Even as young men, they had an idea of what they wanted, while I ran from God and myself. Having experienced a new trio with Argyle and PJ was significant and revealed my desire for closeness and acceptance. I believe God saw my need for structure, wisdom, and protection and provided that in the form of Dusty and Sinclair. These two men poured so much into me and I began to feel humbled.

Clearly, I have been blessed beyond what I deserved and thought about the instances when God's hand spared my life when I showed little value for it. Just like being one of the first in my family to leave home, now I'm the first to leave the P.I. Maybe there is a reason I seem to be first to venture into new territories, maybe I can be one to make a positive difference instead of repeating past failures.

One thing for sure running kept me tired and unsettled. I realized that I needed rest and yearned for stability. But, in order to get a different result, I had to be willing to do something different and as Dusty said it was time for me to live up to my full potential. As I sat on the plane alone, I finally realized that in my life, I couldn't run away from myself.

When I'd had the opportunity to stand and fight, the opportunity to be a man who cries out from within to be heard, I didn't take it, and I continued to run from situation to situation. At this moment, alone on the plane, I could hear my heart scream, "Yes, stand, and be a man." Time has a way of revealing if we are true to ourselves.

As I reflected on these thoughts, the plane rose from the ground, the gravity of my life's situations got the best of me and I wept openly. Not out of sadness or joy but more as a release from all that I held within for so long. I reflected on an adventurous past, while now on a journey into a new and uncertain future with a childlike wonder. What will the next chapters of my life hold for me? While I didn't have any answers, I again affirmed to myself never to run away from me again.

About the Author

Anthony Brinkley served 28 years in the United States Air Force, holding a variety of leadership positions, leading over 100,000 people over his career. He also is one that is deeply involved in his local community. He is the recipient of the 2003 Dr. Martin Luther King Jr. Humanitarian Award for community activities in Tampa Bay, Florida. He is now the CEO of On The Brink Consulting, a company that provides life-changing resilience training to a wide spectrum of individuals and groups.

He answered the call from God and became an ordained minister, spreading concepts of spiritual development through biblically based teaching. Anthony, a former Joint Base Andrews command chief, for a series of leadership development seminars with a specialized emphasis on resiliency. Brinkley's seminars provide teams with the tools to sustain themselves in the midst of challenging situations, while also providing organizational leaders enhanced capabilities to manage and support those they are entrusted to lead.

Anthony has dedicated countless hours to helping those near and far. His activities include counseling local young men on the challenges of life to organizing clothing drives for orphans living in other countries.

He resides in Tampa, Florida.